The County Federations of the Women's Institute

The sixty-nine County Federations are represented on these
[...]ion of their badges, some
[...] the WI archives, vintage.

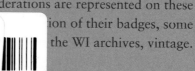

Women's Century

Women's Century

AN ILLUSTRATED HISTORY OF THE WOMEN'S INSTITUTE

Val Horsler & Ian Denning

Third Millennium
Publishing

First published in Great Britain in
2015 by Third Millennium Publishing,
an imprint of Profile Books Ltd

3 Holford Yard
Bevin Way
London WC1X 9HD
United Kingdom
www.tmiltd.com

A CIP catalogue record for this book is
available from The British Library.

ISBN: 978 1 908990 50 1
e-ISBN: 978 1 908990 74 7

Text: Val Horsler
Picture editing, design and layout: Ian Denning
Production: Debbie Wayment
Proofreader: Margaret Histed
Indexer: Elizabeth Wiggans

Reprographics by Tag Publishing, London
Printed and bound by Gorenjski tisk storitve,
Slovenia, on acid-free paper from sustainable
forestry

Picture acknowledgement and credits

The majority of the archive photographs are from the WI Archive
at the Women's Library of the London School of Economics.
The publisher would like to extend its thanks to Anna Towlson
of the London School of Economics Library and Charlotte Fiander
of the NFWI for their invaluable assistance.

The publisher would also like to thank the officers of the FWIs
and WIs who contributed images and information – too many to
list individually here, but they know who they are.

In the list of picture credits below, every effort has been made to
contact the copyright owners of all the images featured in the book.
In the case of an inadvertent omission, please contact Third
Millennium Publishing.

Mat Banks 60–1; Bassano Studio Ltd 20; © Estate of Bertram Park
21; Central Press Photos Ltd/Getty Images 12–13, 86–7, 96–7;
Jacky Chapman 70; Geo T Crouch 78–9; *Daily Mirror* 81 (bottom),
120; Val Doone/Getty Images 77 (bottom); *Eastern Daily Press* 98
(top); *Essex County Standard* 158–9; Elliot Franks 45; *Gloucester
Citizen* 122 (bottom); Ronald Goodearl/thanks to Newsquest
Media Group UK front cover, 162–3; Paul Groom 71; George
W Hales/Fox Photos/Getty Images 76; Daniel Hambury/Stella
Pictures 25, back cover (right); Jackson Hammond 129; Louise
Haywood-Schiefer 53; © David Hedges SWNS.com 24; Thurston
Hopkins/Getty Images 102; © 2010 EO Hoppé Estate Collection/
Curatorial Assistance Inc/National Portrait Gallery, London 23;
Hulton-Deutsch Collection/Corbis 80 (top); Ronald Startup/
Hulton Press Ltd/Picture Post/Getty Images 138–9; Kurt Hutton/
Picture Post/Getty Images 8, 154–5; Chris Jackson/Getty Images
98–9; *Kent Messenger* 169 (bottom); Keystone Press Agency Ltd
46–7, 85 (top), 147; R Kipps 179 (top); Andy Lane 14–15, 22–3,
88–9, 174–5; *Leamington Spa Courier* 166–7; photographs by
Terry Logan 72, 73; Hayley Madden 50–1, 56, 57, 58 (both), 58–9;
Fred Morley/Fox Photos/Getty Images 84; W Dennis Moss 82–3;
Tiffany Mumford/John Brown Media 182; PA/PA Archive/PA
Images 62, 94; Picture Post/Hulton Archive/Getty Images 169 (top);
Paul Reid 180–1; Charles Sainsbury-Plaice 92, 92–3; Camilla
Seymour 186–7; Ronald Startup/Getty Images 160–1; *Sussex
Daily News* 118–19; Mario Testino © 6; J W Thomas 26–7, 100,
106–7, 114 (all), 115, 122 (top), 122–3, 124–5, 127, 128–9; Vintage
Images/Getty Images 164 (bottom); Paul Webb 177; Iain Weir 105,
176–7; N Williams 49 (top).

CONTENTS

MARIO TESTINO ©

It gives me enormous pleasure to write the foreword for this centenary history of the Women's Institute. There is so much to celebrate in the first hundred years of this unique organisation that it is hard to know where to start!

The WI had its beginnings in rural Britain to encourage countrywomen to contribute to the war effort by growing and preserving food. From the establishment of the first WI in 1915, women rose to the challenge and the movement very quickly gathered speed. By the end of 1919, the National Federation of Women's Institutes had been established.

If the Women's Institute began as part of the Home Front, it soon took on a much wider role of its own as the women who joined relished the opportunities it offered. The WI gave women a chance to work together in different ways, contributing to the life of the nation through practical skills, but it also gave them a voice to campaign on the issues that really mattered to the membership. This was true at the beginning and remains so today.

This remarkable women's organisation has achieved so much over the last ten decades. It played its part, helping to feed the country, in the dark days of two World Wars. It gave many women their first taste of working together and encouraged them to use that experience in the wider world. It offered them skills, companionship and confidence in a society where women were still proving themselves as useful citizens. It gave women from all backgrounds a say in campaigns – from equal pay to climate change, from saving the honey bee to legal aid reform for victims of domestic violence.

Today, we can all look back on the last 100 years of our organisation with pride. It has held true to its rural roots and practical skills, but now draws its growing membership from cities as well as counties, from the young as well as the more experienced. As a member of both the Tetbury and Llandovery WI, I am proud to be part of the largest voluntary women's organisation in the country and look forward to the next 100 years, confident that it has so much to offer today's modern woman.

Camilla

PREFACE

Julie Summers

I am honoured and delighted to have been asked to write a short preface for this beautiful book charting the WI's centenary in words and pictures. When I was first approached to write a book about the extraordinary work carried out by the WI during the Second World War I had imagined a history of its agricultural and preserving contribution to the nation's larder. What I discovered was far more interesting, varied, and ambitious: an organisation that mobilised its membership to contribute in every conceivable way to keep the countryside ticking over during the six years of the war while continuing to educate and offer support and friendship. This latter is in some ways the most impressive aspect of the WI both then and now. Women living often isolated lives, certainly in the earliest days of its existence, could and did blossom in a WI. It offered an opportunity to mix with women from different backgrounds with whom they might otherwise have had no reason to cross paths. For Edith Jones, for instance, the arrival of the WI in Smethcote in 1931 was a revelation. Like all women of her generation who lived off the land, her days were filled with preserving the farm and garden produce as well as running the home and caring for her men. But once a month she could escape to join the thirty or so members of Smethcote WI; and by the end of the decade Edith had taken part in and won county-wide baking and handicraft competitions and had been to London for the 1938 AGM. None of this would have happened without the WI.

Nowadays those constraints seem archaic but the spirit of opportunity, companionship, and a safe place to try something different has not changed. It is this combination that makes the WI such an important part of members' lives. When the late Sybil Norcott talked to me about her seventy-two years as a member, she said, 'You'll never be able to sum up the WI in one word. The WI is a way of life.' She was right. And it is a way of life that has a distinguished past and a great future. I salute the Women's Institutes with admiration and affection.

Left: The WI's typical warm greeting, 1950s.

Following pages:
10–11: Community singing, Flamstead (Herts) WI, *c.*1947.
12–13: Enthusiastic voting at the 1971 AGM.
14–15: Delegates at the 2014 Annual Meeting.

Edith Rigby

A founding member of one of the first Women's Institutes in Lancashire, Edith Rigby (1872–1948) was also a militant suffragette who marched on Parliament with the Pankhursts, was imprisoned seven times, went on hunger strike, and was subjected to force-feeding. An early advocate of education for women – a constant theme in the history of the Women's Institute – she founded a school in her home town, Preston (Lancashire), for the education of the women and girls who worked in the local mills. Later, in support of women's suffrage, she planted a pipe bomb at the Liverpool Cotton Exchange, burnt down Lord Leverhulme's bungalow, set fire to Blackburn Rovers' football ground, and hurled acid over a golf course. And this powerful, combative woman was a Women's Institute pioneer, calling it 'a pillar supporting the temple of national enlightenment'.

The first English WI opened just two months later in Sussex, and two years later, in 1917, Sussex became the first county to form its own Federation. By then the movement had spread rapidly, and by the end of 1917 there was a National Federation with a chairman – Gertrude (Trudie) Denman was the first – and a constitution. Its structure, which persists to this day, was in place: the individual – and independent – village WIs, the County Federations which supported them, and the National Federation which provided overall coordination and guidance.

Rural women flocked to join these new communities – often in the teeth of husbandly opposition – which offered them the chance to hear talks and discussions, to learn new crafts or refine their own skills, to raise funds to help causes close to their hearts, and to make new friends and enjoy social occasions. They had to learn quickly how to find and equip suitable meeting places, how to run meetings, how to establish democratic decision-making processes, and how to attract and organise events. The local lady of the manor or wife of a bigwig would often be elected chairman, but the WI was open to all classes of society, and its democratic ideals and female focus sometimes caused flutterings among those accustomed to command and ordain.

The end of the war brought a change of focus but no loss of momentum. In 1919 the National Federation became completely self-governing; Lady Denman announced to the AGM that year that 'the greatest achievement of the Institutes is that we have learnt to govern ourselves. We do not believe in dictators; we believe that each member should be responsible for her Institute and should have a share in the work.' Early moves to affiliate the WI to other organisations, and to make it part of a system of voluntary societies open also to men, were firmly seen off. By the end of 1919, a mere four years after the first WI was established in Anglesey, there were 1,405 Institutes in England and Wales. And that energetic year also saw the establishment of the WI's own magazine, *Home and Country*, which continued to be published until 2006, when it was replaced by *WI Life*.

The WI was fortunate, moreover, in the calibre of its early leaders. Trudie Denman was to guide its progress for three decades, and was ably assisted in the early years by Grace Hadow, a formidable scholar and the intellectual backbone of the movement, and Helena Auerbach, who exercised her powerful business brain as treasurer. All three had been active in the women's suffrage movement, Helena Auerbach as vice-chairman of the Jewish League for Women's Suffrage. Lady Denman was also the first chairman of the Family Planning Association and, during the Second World War, director of the Women's Land Army.

It can fairly be said that the success and longevity of the Women's Institute owe a great deal to the strength of will and foresight of its early protagonists, who clearly saw that it needed to be sensibly structured, self-governing, and

Grace Hadow.
NFWI vice chairman 1919–1940, wearing academic dress, *c.*1919.

A BRIEF HISTORY

Introduction

How to sum up, or categorise, the Women's Institute? Not an easy task, since its public image and the reality of its activities and achievements over the century since it was first established in Great Britain in 1915 are sometimes in conflict. Old photos in sepia or black and white show countrywomen in hats, tending livestock, making cakes and preserves, often apparently middle-aged and perhaps blue-rinsed. 'Jam and Jerusalem' is seen as its watchword. Mention the WI and the perception is of conservative (with both a small and a large 'c'), predominantly village-based, middle-class women.

There is truth in these images. But the other side of the coin is the extraordinary reach and influence that the movement exerted right from the beginning. The WI has carried out a vast amount of campaigning, of lobbying, of highlighting injustices and inequities. Its members collectively make up a pressure group far larger and stronger than many of the major trades unions; its outspokenness about social conditions has led to fundamental changes in the lives of ordinary citizens; its insistence right from the start on a fully democratic and impartial approach to its governance has empowered its membership and given strength to its dealings with authority on all levels; its independence, again asserted from the start, frees it from reliance on others. It has been a force for change, for modernisation, and for the rights of women, but without stridency or nastiness. And as it enters its second century, the WI is constantly changing again, adapting itself to today's world and making itself as relevant to today's women as its first manifestations were to its pioneer members in 1915.

It was a forward-thinking Canadian woman called Adelaide Hoodless who, in the late 1890s, started a movement aimed at educating women in household science and child-rearing. As a mother mourning the loss of a child through contaminated milk, she was determined to stop others suffering the same tragedy, and realised that her best weapon was education. The movement she started grew rapidly in

The traditional image.
Left: A Women's Institute flower and produce stall in Saffron Walden, Essex, 1940s.

LLANFAIRPWLL WOMENS' INSTITUTE, ANGLESEY. SEPT. 1915.
THE FIRST STARTED IN GREAT BRITAIN.

Canada, and was brought to Britain at around the time of the outbreak of the Great War by an energetic Canadian Women's Institute member, Margaret (Madge) Watt. It was an auspicious time for such an initiative, based as it was primarily in rural communities. The explosion of industry in the nineteenth century, which had brought growth and prosperity – along with slums and deep poverty – to cities and towns, had conspired with increasingly cheap imports from abroad to impoverish and denude the countryside. Mrs Watt initially struggled to make her voice heard; but a perhaps unlikely platform for the nascent movement came in the form of a self-help farming society, the Agricultural Organisation Society, founded in 1901, which included among its officers some enlightened men who foresaw the potential of energising rural women. Its secretary, John Nugent Harris, who was a progressive dairy farmer, and the chairman of its North Wales branch, Colonel Richard Stapleton-Cotton, actively encouraged the initiative. A further incentive after the outbreak of war in 1914 was the need to help the war effort. The result was the establishment on September 16 1915 of the first British Women's Institute at Llanfairpwll in Anglesey, north Wales, with Mrs Stapleton-Cotton as its first president. Her husband and his dog Tinker are the only two males ever to have been admitted into full WI membership.

Britain's first WI.
The modest building in Llanfairpwll, Anglesey.

Madge Watt.
Shown wearing the uniform of the Voluntary County Organisers, 1918.

Lady Denman.
Studio portrait by the society
photographer Bertram Park, 1933.

Jerusalem

If there is yet another link between the women's suffrage movement of the first decades of the twentieth century and the Women's Institute, it is to be found in the WI's unofficial anthem, *Jerusalem*. It was Grace Hadow who first suggested in the early 1920s that the song would be a suitable one to be sung at the next AGM. There was some controversy over the choice: 'What woman nowadays yearns for bows, arrows, spears, and chariots of fire?' raged one correspondent in *Home and Country*. 'Boadicea might have done.' But the majority agreed that it was indeed appropriate, and it has been enthusiastically sung ever since at WI meetings.

The WI's roots in the 'green and pleasant land' denuded both by war and by the 'dark Satanic mills' of industrialisation are perhaps sufficient in themselves to proclaim the relevance of William Blake's poem to the organisation. But there is an even closer link in that the Women's Institute actually owned the copyright in Sir Hubert Parry's setting of William Blake's poem from 1928 until 1968, when the music came into the public domain.

Parry initially set the poem to music for organ and voice in response to a request from a patriotic group, Fight for Right, established in 1916 when the country was at a low wartime ebb. Its first conductor was Sir Walford Davies. But Parry was unhappy with the ultra-patriotism of Fight for Right, and withdrew his support and his permission to use the song. However, it had also been taken up in 1917 by the suffragette movement, and when Millicent Garrett Fawcett of the National Union of Women's Suffrage Societies asked him whether her organisation could sing it at a concert in March 1918, Parry was delighted. He not only orchestrated it for the concert but afterwards assigned its copyright to the NUWSS, who owned it until 1928 when, after the group was disbanded following legislation establishing universal suffrage, his executors reassigned it to the Women's Institute.

Its first WI performance at the AGM in 1924 was specially arranged for a string orchestra by Sir Walford Davies, and it was sung by a choir of WI members conducted by W H Leslie. Leslie himself went on to advise and teach singing to a number of WIs, and also wrote articles on music for *Home and Country*.

Above: WI members
singing *Jerusalem* at the
2014 Annual Meeting in
Leeds. *Below*: Composer
Sir Hubert Parry, 1915.

independent. They were also vehement about the need to be
non-sectarian and non-party-political, a stance that was
written into the constitution. Just as they welcomed members
from every class of society, so they firmly kept any form of
partisanship at bay. Members were free to belong to any other
groupings they wished, religious and political, but in their
membership of the WI they left their individual beliefs at
home. They were frequently criticised for their insistence on
this part of the constitution, particularly during the Second
World War when they remained resolutely pacifist, though
always prepared to help humanitarian war work. It was only
in the second half of the twentieth century that the stance was
modified slightly, in order to allow members greater freedom
of discussion about matters of concern to them – though with
the proviso that 'the views and rights of minorities are
respected and… the movement is never used for party
political or sectarian propaganda'. It was this part of the WI
ethos that was the downfall of Tony Blair when he addressed
them in 2000 (*see page 70*).

The WI's early and continuing focus on education came to
triumphant fruition in 1948 when the organisation launched
its own college for adult education. Denman College in
Oxfordshire, named after Lady Denman who was present at
the opening ceremony, continues to this day to offer a wide
variety of courses, some based on traditional WI skills like
crafts and cookery, and others aimed at broadening minds
and enhancing lifestyles. Campaigning too has been at the
heart of WI activity right from the outset, on a huge range of
issues, some surprisingly controversial. Although the more
strident forms of feminism have never found a home within
the Institutes, women's issues have clearly always been at the
forefront of discussion and encouragement, and the insistence
still on all-women membership maintains that focus.

It was perhaps inevitable that the increased freedom
enjoyed by women in the second half of the twentieth century
and the first decades of the twenty-first led to feelings in some

Members of the Wellington WI writing group holding copies of their book.

The WI? Raunchy?

When members of the Wellington (Somerset) WI formed a writing group, they decided to tackle a different genre of literature each month. The results appeared in early 2015 in a book sold to raise funds for the cancer treatment unit at a hospital in Taunton. One of the contributions was a story written after the group had decided one month to focus on erotica, in the mould of the best-selling novel *Fifty Shades of Grey*. Reactions to 'The conquering Gibraltarian Adonis' have ranged from pleased enjoyment to deep shock at its smuttiness. 'It's not for the faint-hearted', said one member of the Wellington WI, and others have expressed horror that something so raunchy should appear in a WI publication. Indeed, they have refused to identify which of their members wrote it, since, as its author has said anonymously, 'my gran would be furious'. And the *Times* journalist who featured it in a piece published on February 12 2015 remarked that it was impossible to reproduce much of it in the newspaper 'without risking elevation to the newsagent's top shelf'.

quarters that the Women's Institute had had its day, that it had less relevance in the modern world where women's rights were enshrined in law and fully accepted in society. And indeed there was a decline in membership during the 1980s and 1990s. But there is now a noticeable resurgence, as women recognise the advantages of a community where skills can be exchanged, ideas discussed, and friendships made. The WI used to be predominantly rural; it is now spreading into the towns and cities, and recruiting younger women who enjoy and benefit from the experience of being part of a group of congenial, supportive, like-minded people. In its centenary year, the Women's Institute is blooming.

The non-traditional image. Jazz Mellor (*right*) and members of the Shoreditch Sisters WI craft group, knitting at 'Time for Tea' on Shoreditch High Street, London, 2011.

The original emblem.
A Canadian quilt with a maple leaf design incorporating the WI's emblem, a gift to Denman College, 1954.

1915 Llanfairpwll WI – the first WI meeting.

1917 Talybont WI – butter- and cheese-making class.

1920s Chidham WI – meeting at Cobnor.

*c.***1920** Kemsing WI – outing to Hastings.

1924 Billesdon WI – summer picnic at Miss Belgrove's, Skeffington.

1925 Lampeter WI – Lady Lisburne Challenge Cup.

1928 Bwlchllan WI.

1920s Abinger WI.

*c.***1930** Rydes Hill WI – outing to the Houses of Parliament.

1930s Pirbright WI – river trip.

1935 Market Bosworth WI – second anniversary of its founding.

1954 Whittington District WI – costumes spanning seven centuries.

1967 Billesdon WI – outing to Campbell's soup factory.

1982 Ranskill and Torworth WI – visit to Harworth Colliery.

2009 Colchester WIGs – the 'Women's Institute Girls'.

2010 Dilton Marsh WI – Wiltshire winners of the NFWI's 'WI Tri' triathlon event.

CAMPAIGNING

Chapter 1

Right from the outset, the Annual General Meeting of the Women's Institute considered 'resolutions' brought to it by its members, which were discussed and – if agreed – redefined as 'mandates'. And right from the outset, these resolutions and mandates have covered a wide range of topics, not just the concerns of immediate interest to the largely rural membership, but support for national and women's issues as well. The establishment of a mandate has inevitably been followed by targeted, focused, and energetic lobbying of successive governments in the last century, and they have grown used to firm pressure put on them by this influential and powerful women's group. The vision of its founders in insisting on independence, democracy, and non-partisanship bore immediate fruit in the strength and authority such insistence allowed it to wield.

Moreover, the democratic ethos within which resolutions and mandates were, and still are, submitted, debated, and agreed was designed to ensure that the voice of every member of every WI can be heard nationally. It is the members who decide on the organisation's policy and the campaigns it supports and fights for. Neither the National Federation nor the County Federations have a voice separate from the collective voices of the Institutes and their members nationwide.

A 1921 issue of *Home and Country* saw clearly that the NFWI would become a real power in the land: 'If one person alone cannot make her wants heard it becomes much easier when there are numbers wanting the same kind of things.' This quickly showed itself to be true; and the WI's campaigning heft is no less well recognised today among politicians and pressure groups. Theresa May, the Conservative Home Secretary, speaking in July 2014, noted that the WI had always been 'renowned for its vigorous campaigning... you have a formidable reputation for standing your ground and showing just what can be achieved when people come together to get things done.' And even while he

Campaigning.
Two generations of WI campaigners in Trafalgar Square, 2008.

Getting things done.
A light-hearted poster published by the Surrey FWI, 1948.

was in other ways hitting the wrong note in his speech to the AGM in 2000, Tony Blair applauded the WI as 'a very powerful force for good in our country... a great tribute to the depth of your compassion, your fearlessness in tackling hard issues, and the energy with which you further the cause of not just women but British society'.

Women's rights

It is to be expected that women's rights have always been a prominent focus for the WI. At the end of the First World War women were enfranchised in a limited way, though votes for all women had to wait until 1928. The WI – as opposed, however, to some of its prominent founder members – did not involve itself directly in the suffrage movement; but it was determined that women, as citizens, should play their full part in national affairs. In 1921, the year after women had first been allowed to serve as jurors, the Surrey Federation proposed a resolution at the AGM that all qualified women should be urged to recognise their responsibility to serve as jurors if summoned and not to seek exemption. It was a subject to which the WI was to return, particularly since the property qualifications for service continued for years to rule out many women. In the 1960s the Home Office and legal groups were extensively lobbied, by the WI and others, about the criteria for jury service; the eventual result was the Juries Act of 1974, which redefined the categories of people who could be called for jury service, and made no distinction between women and men.

Equal pay for equal work was another campaign. In 1943, when the end of the war was in sight and men and women all over the country were turning their attention to how things would and should change in peacetime, the WI at Bures in Suffolk put forward a resolution demanding that men and women doing the same jobs should receive the same pay. The mandate was communicated to government ministries, the trades unions, and employers' organisations, and in 1944 the WI submitted evidence to the Royal Commission on Equal Pay. Lobbying continued, with emphasis in the 1950s on professions such as teaching, until in 1970 the Equal Pay Act enshrined the principle in law. The Act was not implemented until 1976, which gave employers plenty of time to redefine jobs and structures so that they could get round the provisions, and equal pay for equal work is still by no means a universal given. But one may tentatively hope that few major employers today would countenance paying men more than women for doing the same job.

The environment

A memorable campaign by the WI was Keep Britain Tidy, proposed by the Northumberland Federation in 1954 and enthusiastically taken up by the membership at large. The first mandate concerning litter had actually been passed in 1925; but now the WI was joined by a number of other organisations in seeking support and funding from the

The Tidyman logo.
The ubiquitous symbol representing the Keep Britain Tidy campaign.

government for an anti-litter campaign, which was granted in 1957 and allowed the appointment of a full-time secretary who was based in the National Federation's offices. The campaign became fully independent in 1961, when Queen Elizabeth the Queen Mother agreed to become its patron; and the link with the WI continued when in 1966 Elisabeth Brunner, who had been WI chairman in 1954 when it all started, became president. The 1958 Litter Act was attributed largely to Keep Britain Tidy, and during its passage through Parliament MPs praised the WI for its central role in changing public perceptions about litter and transforming policy.

The campaign – encapsulated in its Tidyman logo – has always been supported by a host of high-profile people, as well as by those prolific litter-pickers, the Wombles, and remains a powerful force today. The high profile of Keep Britain Tidy allows it to run a range of programmes aimed at areas like beaches, parks, and rivers, and it offers awards, training schemes, waste watch services, and environmental surveys among other initiatives (Dog Poo Fairy is one example!).

As early as 1927, WI members were concerned about pollution in the sea; and more recently the WI has joined forces with other major campaign groups, like Greenpeace, to lobby on the depletion of the ozone layer and to preserve the natural state of Antarctica. Both of those particular initiatives were followed by the British government signing up to international concordats on the issues. On one day in 2005, WI members nationwide inundated supermarkets with excess packaging as part of a campaign aimed at protecting and conserving natural resources. And the carbon challenge of 2008 saw 10,000 members signing up to reduce their carbon footprint.

A current initiative is SOS for Honey Bees, which has seen members raising awareness of the decline in the honey bee population and doing their best to help combat it by planting bee-friendly gardens – and urging local authorities to do the

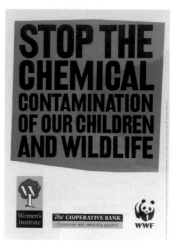

Chemicals and health.
Right: WI members take part in a petition event as part of the Chemicals and Health Campaign at the European Parliament in Strasbourg, 2003.

The next generation -TOXIC !

BAN HAZARDOUS CHEMICALS NOW BEFORE OUR CHILDRENS BODIES ARE HARMED WE NEED YOUR HELP NOW

I CARE ~ WILL YOU?

My son is working with harmful chemicals everyday, I want him to have a safe environment.

Karen Perkins
Fishguard
Pembrokeshire
West Wales

same – as well as taking up bee-keeping themselves. On a national level, the WI has joined with other groups to campaign for central policy changes on this vital issue; the result, in November 2014, was the government's National Pollinator Strategy.

In the early 1990s a group of major campaigning bodies, including the WI, joined together to set up the Fairtrade Foundation, part of a global initiative aimed at ensuring that farmers and workers in the developing world receive fair terms for their produce. Companies who achieve Fairtrade designation pay sustainably better prices, which are never lower than the market price, and campaign for good working conditions. The Foundation licenses and monitors the use of the Fairtrade mark in the UK; there are currently around 4,500 products, worth around £1.7 billion, with the designation, and over a million workers, along with their families and communities in the developing world, have benefited from the changes brought about by the campaign.

The WI in hospitals.

Left: A notice board with a poster showing the date of the next meeting at Fulbourn Hospital, the first Women's Institute to be established for staff and patients in a psychiatric hospital, 1970s.

Health

Controversial health issues have never proved anathema to the WI. As early as 1922, when any discussion of sexually transmitted disease was taboo in polite society, the WI at its AGM welcomed the committee set up that year by the Ministry of Health to tackle the problem, and also urged that 'questions of public health should be given due weight in education'. And just over sixty years later, in 1986, the movement was among the first public bodies to seek to raise awareness of HIV and AIDS, to educate the public about the realities of the disease, and to bring it out from the shadows. WI members joined in both government and BBC initiatives to talk about the subject and try to dispel prejudice. As the Terrence Higgins Trust proclaimed, 'The WI does not flinch from the more difficult issues that face society.'

Compassion has always been at the root of WI work on health matters. In 1938 there were calls for better pay and conditions for nurses, who often worked immensely long hours for little reward. And it is hard now to remember that up until the late 1950s parents were often forbidden to visit their sick children in hospital, in the belief that such visits upset the patients. The Hampshire Federation set out to address this in 1950, proposing a mandate asking hospital managements to allow parental visits that was sent to the Ministry of Health, the regional hospital boards, and hospital management committees. Visiting hours for parents with children in hospital are now almost unrestricted.

Dental care in both 1926 and 1960; breast cancer screening in 1975; smoking in public places in 1964, forty-three years before the ban on smoking in public buildings finally came into force; mandatory family planning services in 1972, including the provision of free contraception regardless of age or marital status – these were some of the health issues adopted and fought for by the Women's Institute.

More recently, a 2014 mandate echoed the movement's concern about organ donation, which it first tackled in 1952,

Sheer common sense

Although the WI has never shied away from discussing, tackling, and lobbying on major issues of national importance, it has also always sought to deal with the smaller inconveniences and inequities that life throws up. In 1921 members were urged to support the principles of what became the Plumage Act of 1922, which forbade the import of the feathers of exotic birds. And they returned to animal welfare issues in the 1950s when they campaigned for better conditions for horses being transported overseas, and in 1970 when they appealed for legislation to prohibit the killing of badgers except by special licence; the result was the 1973 Badgers Act.

In 1946 attention was drawn to the inadequacy of lavatories at railway stations, and the need for the provision on long-distance trains of a place where mothers with babies could change nappies in privacy. And in 1956, members started a campaign against turnstiles in women's public lavatories, which discriminated against the elderly, pregnant, and disabled; a 1963 Act of Parliament forbade their installation in new facilities.

Why should purchase tax, and later VAT, be levied on the cooking and housework tools essential for what, in 1957, was seen as mainly women's work, when the tools of a man's trade carried no such extra imposition? Why should the younger members of hard-working families be subjected to violence in all its lurid details in some sections of the press? Please would the manufacturers of fireworks be aware of the dangers inherent in their products and take more care in their sale? Such have been the everyday concerns of Women's Institute members, who have brought their own experiences and worries to the AGM and seen them adopted as mandates to be discussed and fought for among the membership at large. And such has been the fearsome campaigning reputation of the WI among the governing classes that they have almost invariably realised that they have no choice other than to listen and to act.

Care Not Custody Coalition.
Home Secretary Theresa May
speaking at a Care Not Custody
Coalition event, July 2014.

when corneal grafting was still not legal in the UK; all WI
members are now urged to make their own wishes clear on
this issue, and to encourage family and friends to do the same.
And a 2012 mandate built on past concerns about the
provision of midwives by calling for More Midwives and
improvements in care for pregnant women and their families.
The findings of an investigation into women's childbirth
experiences have found their way into the Parliamentary
Public Accounts Committee Report and the NHS Chief
Executive's five year forward plan. New guidance on safe
staffing for maternity wards has been developed, and
maternity staffing was firmly on the agenda in the 2015 general
election with a number of party commitments on the issue.

Mental health too is on the agenda, specifically in one 2008
mandate on the care of people with mental problems who
come into contact with the criminal justice system. After the
tragic suicide, while imprisoned, of the schizophrenic son of a
Norfolk member, the WI joined forces with the Prison
Reform Trust and a number of other organisations concerned
with mental health issues in what eventually became the Care
Not Custody Coalition, aimed at demonstrating the breadth
of support for more effective arrangements across the country
for people with mental health needs and learning disabilities
caught up in the criminal justice system. The campaign
succeeded in obtaining government backing and funding for
pilot schemes to ensure that treatment and support are
available for vulnerable people who need them, and extracted
promises from government that national liaison and diversion
service pilots would be trialled.

'The WI does not flinch from the more difficult issues'

– The Terrence Higgins Trust

Delegation on their way to present a petition of 600,000 signatures to 10 Downing Street following the NFWI resolution on Equal Pay for Equal Work. Left to right: Dr Edith Summerskill, Patricia Ford, Barbara Castle, and Irene Ward, 1954.

Keep Britain Tidy.
The message of a 1954 WI
group *(left)* campaigning to
Keep Britain Tidy is reprised
(above) by a twenty-first century
group of campaigners, with
a sculpture of a Tidyman
logo made of black rubbish
behind them.

Local campaigns.

Above: Lisvane WI members
clear litter for 'Keep Britain
Tidy' while local binmen
look on, Glamorgan, 1983.
Right: 'Hyde Heath WI Litter
Drive in Progress' – cleaning up
the village as part of their
campaign, 1976.

Excessive packaging.
WI members, on one day in
2005, targeted supermarkets all
over the country by dumping
excess packaging materials.

Violence against women.

Left: The patchwork 'Map of Gaps' quilt, conceived by the NFWI as a protest against the patchy provision of support services for women victims of violence, particularly in rural areas. The completed quilt, designed and sewn together by Shoreditch Sisters WI, was presented as a petition to Parliament in 2009. *Above*: Marylyn Haines Evans speaking at a rally outside the Supreme Court to protest against legal aid reforms, and their disproportionate impact on women who experience violence, 2011.

Mayfield Evening WI.

St Stephen WI.

Hawkesbury and Horton WI.

Cottenham WI.

Rhayader WI.

Busy bees.

WI members and friends, in a variety of costumes, taking part in their local carnivals for the national SOS for Honeybees Campaign, 2009.

Bromham WI.

Milking the publicity.

Left and above: Two WI members campaigning in 2007 to highlight the low price paid to farmers for their milk. The milk bath in Parliament Gardens was staged to publicise the handing over of a petition on the issue to Caroline Spelman MP.

90@90 campaign.

WI members across the country joined enthusiastically in the 90@90 campaign to promote efficient waste recycling. A group (above) from Freshney WI are pictured standing in front of a rubbish compactor on a landfill site, during a visit to the Energy from Waste facility at Stallingborough, Lincolnshire, 2007.

Raising the standard.

Left: The WI section of the Climate March in London, September 21 2014.

Above: Flying the WI flag at the Stop Climate Chaos Coalition's No New Coal protest at Kingsnorth power station, 2008.

PUBLIC AFFAIRS

Chapter 2

The establishment in Britain of the first Women's Institutes during the Great War came about because those first WI members saw their new communities as a means towards improving their own lives and their immediate environment; the pioneers of Llanfairpwll set themselves 'to do our utmost to make the village the centre of good in our neighbourhood'. Rooted in the tragedy of a child dying because of ignorance about contaminated milk, the movement quickly became ferocious about seeking education, knowledge, and training in the skills and crafts of rural life.

Yet the Institutes were being established in the context of a brutal and bruising war, and it was also true that the involvement of the women at home while the men were at the front was seen as a huge boost to the war effort, both in upholding morale and, more directly, in helping to feed the country. As the war drew to an end, it is clear that the efforts of women in wartime, WI members and others, were recognised by the male establishment as an essential part of the ultimate victory: even while fighting continued, in 1918, new legislation granted votes to (some) women and allowed women to be elected to Parliament. The WI was therefore, right from its beginnings, more than just a conglomeration of women's groups doing women's things; it was always there at the edges of central policy-making. And as its strength grew, it became – and has remained to this day – a force to be reckoned with in the public arena.

Wartime

In 1914 Britain produced only 35% of its own food, and a major German initiative during the war was therefore to starve the country into surrender by attacking ships importing food from abroad. This blockade was so successful that, at the end of April 1917, there was only six weeks' worth of food reserves left in the country.

The newly formed WIs threw themselves into the task of increasing food production, both by educating themselves in

Annual General Meeting.
Mrs J Marshall of the Stokenchurch (Bucks) WI addressing delegates at the Royal Albert Hall, 1970.

more efficient agricultural methods and by ensuring that no food went to waste. One institute increased its small village's yield of potatoes by eleven and a half tons one year, and in general, huge efforts were made to preserve fruit by bottling it and making jam, to grow vegetables, to gather herbs for both medicinal and culinary use, to keep hens for egg production, and to breed rabbits for the pot. By the end of the war in 1918, Britain's self-sufficiency in food was over 60%, and it was recognised by the government that the WI had made a huge contribution to this achievement, so much so that they awarded it an annual grant of £10,000.

Right at the start of the Second World War, the Ministry of Agriculture called on the WIs again to turn their efforts to ensuring that no fruit or vegetables went to waste. They were invited to establish a Cooperative Fruit Preservation Scheme, and were supplied with preserving and canning equipment imported from America. *Home and Country* urged its readers to throw themselves into the scheme, pronouncing that 'Produce – preserve' must be their watchwords, and supplying recipes for preserving fruit without sugar. Preserving centres and canning factories were set up in village halls and farm buildings, and by the end of 1940 some three and a half million pounds of fruit had been processed, much of which might in other circumstances have been wasted. On one day alone in Somerset, a glut of cherries was picked and transformed into 780 pounds of jam and canned fruit.

All the labour provided by WI members was free, and they often disregarded air-raid warnings as they refused to leave their jam cooking while taking shelter. One group of five women in the east Kent village of Hawkinge, in constant danger during the Battle of Britain from warring aircraft overhead, stayed to stir their jam and bottle their fruit during the heaviest of raids, producing in 1940 nearly 800 pounds of jam and 900 cans and bottles of fruit. When jam jars ran short, village Institutes organised trips to the rubbish tips of large cities to scavenge for suitable containers. And one village

Wartime canning.
A demonstration of how to use a Dixie Hand Sealing Machine to preserve fruit, 1940.

Not a 'cannon' factory.
Queen Elizabeth visiting a WI
canning unit at Reading, 1942.

in Buckinghamshire suffered a targeted bombing raid after
Lord Haw Haw announced in his broadcast that Queen
Elizabeth had visited a 'cannon' factory there.

Rabbits, hens, goats, and pigs were bred. Herbs were
gathered mainly for the manufacture of medicinal drugs: rose
hips for vitamin C syrup, foxglove leaves for heart medicine.
Recipes designed both to eke out scarce ingredients and to
utilise foraged plants like stinging nettles were published.
Wool was gathered from hedgerows, clothes were sewn and
knitted for the troops and for refugees, scrap iron and waste
paper were collected.

Throughout it all, in accordance with the non-sectarianism
that was enshrined in its constitution – and in deference to its
Quaker members – the Women's Institute refused to engage in
civil defence and other types of direct war work. Its efforts
were however hugely important in feeding everyone, keeping
morale high, and generally putting its members' considerable
strengths into supporting the war-torn people of Britain. And
perhaps one of its most high-profile involvements was with
children, and often their mothers, evacuated from city centres
vulnerable to bombing.

Evacuation plans were among the earliest to be put in place
during the final years of the 1930s when war loomed ever
more closely; and it was the Women's Institute to whom the
government first turned on this issue. As early as September
1938, during the Munich crisis, the small department in the
Home Office dealing with evacuation was so overwhelmed
with enquiries that they borrowed a typist and a typewriter
from the National Federation. Things moved very quickly;
within a few days, WI county volunteers were contacted
to start to consider how the scheme would work, and
also within a few days they were asked to extend their
plans to include babies and children under the age of five.
A contingent of children from London were actually sent
to Cambridge, but were promptly sent back when Neville
Chamberlain returned from Munich announcing that he

believed he had secured a deal which would ensure 'peace for our time'.

During that hectic week the WI had shown that it could respond very quickly and effectively when called upon. It took merely hours for places to be found to take the children, crèches to be arranged, and equipment rounded up. When war was finally declared a year later, evacuation procedures were in the hands of the Women's Voluntary Service, but it was still down to hundreds of WI members in the countryside to receive, home, and care for the evacuees. During three days, nearly one and a half million mothers and children filled trains, buses, and even paddle steamers leaving London and other cities for the country.

That first exodus didn't last very long. Once it seemed clear that the expected bombing raids were not likely to happen immediately, many returned to their urban homes. But there was a second wave in 1940 after the fall of France, which included families from the coastal towns of the south-east where invasion seemed most likely.

The influx of urban dwellers into rural communities inevitably caused major cultural clashes. Many of the children came from deprived city areas and were riven with head lice and scabies. Some of them had little or no toilet training, and simply relieved themselves where they happened to be. The food was unfamiliar, the countryside was strange and lonely, there were no cinemas or neighbourly gossip. Rural and urban ways of life simply did not always mix, and those who could not adapt quickly returned home, including a large proportion of the evacuated mothers. The stories that emerged after the war included hostile hosts, reluctant guests, an inability to understand each other; but on the other side of the coin were warm welcomes, children who settled in happily in an atmosphere of love and acceptance, and new, lifelong friendships.

It was typical of the Women's Institute that it should use the experience to draw conclusions about conditions for the

A record of the war.
Title page of the hand-drawn Dorset FWI War Record 1939–1945. The beautifully illustrated entries for Charmouth WI and Durweston WI are shown opposite.

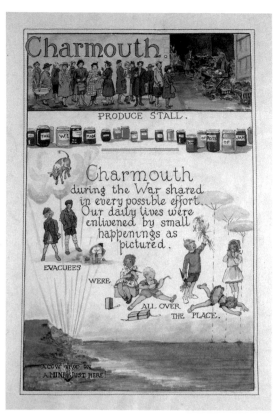

poorer sections of urban society. It did not take long for the organisation to produce a report on what its members had found when hosting evacuee children; published in early 1940, it was titled 'Town children through country eyes', and was based on a survey completed by over 1,700 Institutes. It was the start of a lobbying campaign which eventually led to recommendations about nursery provision and education in slum areas. It also called for financial help for poorer urban families; as a result the 'family allowance' was established after the war.

Relationship with government

The 1960s, famously, saw many changes in society, notably in increased freedom for women to pursue careers, to plan their families, to make choices for themselves that were simply not available to their mothers and grandmothers. The growth of 'women's lib', the advent and wide availability of the contraceptive pill, the increased educational and working opportunities for women – all heralded a sea-change in society. There must have been something in the air in 1967, which saw the decriminalisation of both homosexuality and abortion; equal pay and equal employment rights for women were enshrined in legislation in the early 1970s, which also saw the first previously all-male Oxbridge colleges open themselves to women undergraduates. 'Why would I want to join a college that is closed to half the human race?' was the reaction of one bright young man offered a scholarship to a Cambridge college that was still resisting the admission of women. He was typical of the changing times.

The Women's Institute, as an educational charity, retains to this day its constitutional restriction on men as members, though many of its activities, notably at Denman, are open equally to women and men. However, the changes in society during those turbulent decades, the 1960s and 1970s, had their effect on the WI too, particularly in the increasingly apparent wish of WI members to be free to range more widely

Grabbing the headlines.
A newspaper seller with
copies of the London *Evening
News* carrying the headline
'WI Calls for Action' outside
the Royal Albert Hall at the
time of the AGM, 1978.

in their meetings, and to hold discussions on political and
moral issues. In this they were hampered to some extent by
the strict non-partisan, non-party-political rule that was
enshrined in the constitution.

Those attending the conference called in the early 1970s to
discuss a change to the rule knew that it would be
controversial. Opponents feared that partisan groups might
exploit the WI for their own ends, and that government
would not listen as closely if there was suspicion that the
organisation might be open to pressure. Others worried that
heated discussion might disrupt the friendliness of WI
meetings. But those in favour of change argued that the
emphasis on self-education and broadening of horizons over
the decades should now lead to the ability to tackle difficult
issues, and that the increasing intrusion of government into
everyone's lives required discussion within the WI if it was to
remain relevant and influential. Besides, many groups were
already breaking the rule!

So the change to the constitution was effected, but always
with the proviso that minorities were respected and that the
WI would never allow itself to be used for sectarian or
party-political propaganda.

It was the movement's strict adherence to this principle
that saw the very public humiliation of the Prime Minister,
Tony Blair, when he addressed the AGM in June 2000. In the
immediate aftermath of the gleeful news stories about the
reception he received, there was a difference of opinion about
whether the WI had invited him to speak to them or whether
it had been Downing Street that had made the approach. The
truth was the latter; and Mr Blair had been warned when the
WI agreed that he would be part of the proceedings, that the
Women's Institute would not tolerate an overt party-political
stance.

Downing Street had clearly seen the conference as the ideal
platform from which to reposition New Labour as the
champion of traditional values within a changing world and

The wrong tone.
The Prime Minister,
Tony Blair, addressing the
Women's Institute AGM
at Wembley Arena, 2000,
with NFWI chairman,
Helen Carey, looking on.

in a new century. Tony Blair had just celebrated the birth of
his fourth child and had broken the usual male politician
mould by taking paternity leave. He and his advisers saw the
WI, busily shaking off its image as conservative and fuddy-
duddy, as the perfect audience for a government and a party
seeking similarly to shake off its old image.

The Prime Minister was warmly welcomed when he rose
to speak, and his listeners even reacted with humour when he
told them that they were 'the most terrifying audience' he had
ever faced. They remained polite when he referred to the
recent row about apparent elitism in university admission
policies, which Gordon Brown had exploited to point up
what he claimed was class bias. 'No more class war,' Tony
Blair said; 'we are unashamed supporters of excellence.' But
the trouble began when he moved on to government
initiatives aimed at extending opportunity, regaling the
audience with the achievements of his own party in tackling
the difficulties faced by sectors of society like the disabled and
single parents. As he listed the policies his government had

introduced to help the disadvantaged, heckling started in the section of the hall where delegates from the West Midlands were sitting. When he moved on to NHS reform, the slow handclapping started, and grew in volume until Helen Carey, in the chair, appealed for calm and begged the audience to allow him to finish. It was when the delegates jeered his eulogy about Labour's interest cuts since coming to power in 1997 that he was thrown off his stride.

'Well, I'm glad we are having a good debate,' he said. 'No', was the general response; 'this is a party political broadcast'. And although he won a few plaudits for some of the points he went on to make, the end of his speech was greeted by silence from many of the delegates and merely polite applause from the rest. The debacle made predictable headlines, and was of course seized on by the Conservative opposition. There were red faces all round at Downing Street at this extraordinary political misjudgment; and perhaps predictable surprise in the media that it should have been the Women's Institute that carried out this firm political handbagging.

Ten years later, on June 2 2010, it was John Bercow, the Speaker of the House of Commons, who addressed the AGM, though this time it was by video conferencing – not, as he hastily explained, because 'I have suddenly realised that today is almost ten years to the moment since Tony Blair famously addressed your august body and did not go down that well, leading me to chicken out of appearing in person'. No, it was because the delay in setting up a government following the hung election of May that year meant that parliamentary business did not permit him to leave Westminster for Cardiff, where the AGM was being held.

He went on to say that he was very keen to address them because he saw a number of similarities between the House of Commons and the Women's Institute, and because he felt that certain aspects of the ways in which the WI had transformed itself in recent years could be an exemplar for Parliament, which at the time was still struggling in the wake of the

At a safe distance?
Speaker John Bercow, addressing the AGM via videolink at Cardiff International Arena, 2010.

Calendar Girls

The film, starring Helen Mirren and Julie Walters, that told the story of the calendar produced for the year 2000 by members of the Rylstone and District (Yorkshire) Women's Institute distorted the reality somewhat, particularly by imagining disapproval of the project from both other members of the local WI and the National Federation. Dramatic licence had its way in the film; but the truth was that there was huge support for the idea at both local and national level.

The initiative was the brainchild of Tricia Stewart, whose friend Angela Baker was mourning the sudden death from leukaemia of her husband John. The original aim was to raise money to buy a sofa for the cancer unit where he had been treated. Mrs Stewart and Mrs Baker persuaded nine other women from their WI to join them in posing for a calendar showing them carrying out traditional WI activities such as making jam and cakes and pressing fruit, but naked and with strategically placed props.

They also recruited a retired professional photographer, whose wife was one of the models, to take the photos. John Baker had grown sunflowers, and had hoped to live to see the ones he planted in 1998 come to bloom; sadly his death came too soon, but the flowers he planted formed a theme throughout the calendar.

expenses scandal. 'At a minimum,' he said, 'the WI and the House of Commons share the burden of harsh media stereotyping. It must drive you collectively to madness that the media cannot report your activities without implying, lazily, that your primary purpose is to provide jam today. Parliamentarians, on the other hand, suffer from the slightly less inaccurate media accusation that all we do is promise jam tomorrow.'

Both, he said, were complicated organisations which had to maintain their positions in a changing world. Many groups similar to the WI had faded away as they became out of touch

January 2000

mon	tue	wed	thurs	fri	sat	sun
					1	2
3	4	5	6	7	8	9
10	11	12	13	14	15	16
17	18	19	20	21	22	23
24	25	26	27	28	29	30
31						

Mrs Baker and Mrs Stewart both featured in the calendar, as Miss February playing the piano and Miss October pressing apples. The oldest model, Beryl Bamforth as Miss January, appeared chairing a meeting with the audience wearing nothing but hats. The December image was an ensemble photograph showing all the women singing carols.

The Alternative WI Calendar was released in April 1999 with a small initial print run which sold out within a week. Another run of 10,000 was hastily printed and that took a mere three weeks to sell. By now it was becoming both nationally and internationally famous, and by the end of the year it had sold 88,000 copies. An American edition covering June 2000 to December 2001 sold over 200,000 copies, and there have been several others since, including one for 2004 which also featured some of the stars of the film. The phenomenon continues, with ranges of merchandise and a 2010 reprise of the calendar in colour. A massive amount of money has been raised for leukaemia research at the University of Leeds, where a plaque has been erected in memory of the inspiration for the original calendar, John Baker.

The huge success inspired both a film and a play, with Helen Mirren and Julie Walters nominated for awards, and the film winning best film in the 2003 Comedy Awards. The play opened in 2008 as part of the Chichester Theatre Festival, and subsequently transferred to the West End. It is fair to say that the aftermath caused some tension within Rylstone WI, with five of the original models disassociating themselves from further involvement. However, the calendar has spawned innumerable imitations, with people and communities all over the place baring themselves in the cause of charity.

and irrelevant. Yet the WI had not only survived, but was thriving and 'if it were a political party would [be] at least the second largest in the land'. And it had done this by retaining its traditional values while taking on 'modern, topical, gritty, and challenging social issues'. Respect has to be earned, relevance has to be demonstrated, he said, and he was keen to follow the WI's lead in reaching out beyond the confines of the Westminster bubble to take Parliament to the people. Outreach programmes were being developed, and 'like the WI, I want to take on challenging areas, not merely comfortable ones'.

An ambulance being presented to the army by the WI at their London headquarters in 1940. Dame Frances Farrer, NFWI General Secretary, stands next to Lady Denman, NFWI chairman, and an army officer.

'If it were a political party it would be at least the second largest in the land.'

– *John Bercow, Speaker of the House of Commons, 2010*

Sustenance in wartime.

Left: A WI member ringing the lunch bell at the Priory Evacuated Women's Club in Hitchin, Hertfordshire, where evacuated mothers and their children could meet over a cheap meal, 1939. *Above*: Providing pies as part of the Ministry of Food's 'Meals in Rural Areas' scheme, Toft (Cheshire) WI, Cheshire, 1943. *Right*: British soldiers being offered tea and cakes at a WI dance, *c*.1943.

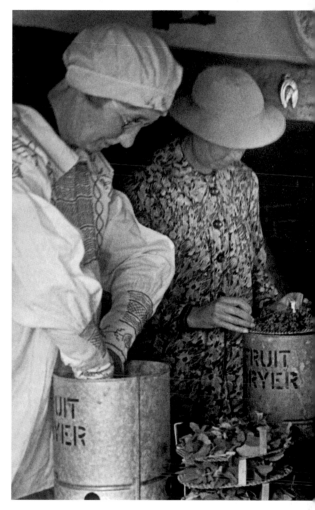

Food preservation.
Left: Members of the Hampshire FWI canning fruit, 1940s. *Above*: Using galvanised fruit dryers to preserve herbs at the Culinary Herb Drying Centre, Sussex, 1941.

Fruit for jam.
Above: Members of the Women's Institute weigh and stone cherries in order to make jam, 1943.
Left: Women picking fruit, Dean (Beds) WI, 1941.

Groaning shelves.

Above: Writing jam jar labels for the store cupboard at Mereworth WI Fruit Preservation Centre, Kent, 1943.
Right: Checking WI canned goods at the Fruit Preservation Store, Barford Depot, Warwickshire, 1942.

Wartime visitors.

Above: Queen Mary visiting Kemble WI Fruit Preservation Centre, Gloucestershire, where women are washing and drying glass jars, 1941. *Right above*: Queen Elizabeth watching WI member Mrs Elizabeth Van Kerckhoven demonstrate fruit canning at Hyde Heath Fruit Preservation Centre, Buckinghamshire, 1940. *Right below*: US First Lady Eleanor Roosevelt inspecting a jar of jam on her visit to the Barham WI Fruit Preservation Centre, East Kent, 1942; Clementine Churchill is in the background on the right.

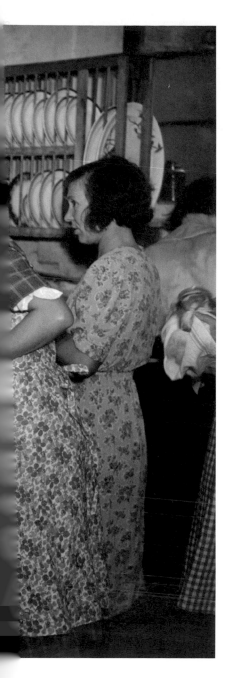

Aid from America.
WI members using a mobile canning
unit presented to them by the British War
Relief Society of America, 1941.

Aid to Russia.

Above: Fur garments made by WI members in support of Clementine Churchill's 'Aid to Russia' scheme, 1942.
Right: Clementine Churchill's letter to Shillingstone WI Fruit Preservation Centre thanking them for their £1 contribution (receipt below), 1942. The letter reads: 'Dear Members, Thank-you very much for your gift which I have just received. I am most grateful to you for the trouble you have taken to help the brave Russians in their terrible struggle and in the glorious defence of their country. Your sincere friend, Clementine S. Churchill.'

March 1942

10, Downing Street,
Whitehall.

Dear Members

Thank - you very much for your gift which I have just received -

I am most grate- -ful to you for the trouble you have

THE MEMBERS OF THE SHILLINGSTONE WOMEN'S
INSTITUTE FRUIT PRESERVATION CENTRE (1941)
per Mrs M.Silverston,   361574
Croft Cottage,
Shillingstone,   17th March, 1942.
Nr.Blandford, Dorset.

This is to acknowledge with grateful thanks your contribution to Mrs. Churchill's Red Cross "Aid to Russia" Fund.

£1. 0.- 0.   W.H.Goschen.
                                         Hon. Treasurer.

This fund is being raised on behalf of the War Organisation of the British Red Cross Society and the
Order of St. John of Jerusalem, registered under the War Charities Act, 1940.

An annual get-together. Delegates to the 1971 AGM at the Royal Albert Hall relax during the lunch break on the steps of the Albert Memorial, Kensington, London.

Delegates.

Above: For delegates from the
Isle of Wight, travelling to the
AGM always involves a ferry
journey; this one was in 1965.
Left: Breaking a Guinness world
record for mass knitting at the
Royal Albert Hall during the
2012 Annual Meeting.

Ladies at the microphone.

Above: Lady Albemarle, chairman 1946–1951, at the 1951 AGM.

Right above: Lady Brunner, chairman 1951–1956, at the 1952 AGM.

Right below: Lady Dyer, chairman 1956–1961, at the 1957 AGM.

The ninetieth anniversary AGM.
Jane Fonda (*above*) addressing the
audience at the Royal Albert Hall (*right*)
as guest speaker at the 2005 AGM.

A 1962 NFWI delegation to the Soviet Union.
Left: Mrs Gabrielle Pike, NFWI chairman (with camera), and Miss Bloxam leaving the plane. *Above*: With a group of Ukrainian women. *Right*: With Ukrainian singers in traditional costume at a cultural centre. *Below*: Helping with blackcurrent-picking on a Ukrainian collective fruit farm run by Galina Burkatskaya (*left*) of the Soviet Women's Committee.

Lost in a sea of hats. HRH The Duke of Edinburgh surrounded by Women's Institute members at the Royal Garden Party at Buckingham Palace to celebrate the WI's Golden Jubilee, 1965.

Four generations of royal WI members.
Left above: The Queen, Queen Mother, and
Princess Margaret arriving for a meeting of the
Sandringham Women's Institute, 1977.
Left below: Queen Elizabeth II at a Sandringham
WI meeting, her first one as monarch, 1953.
Above: The Queen cuts the centenary cake at
the 2015 Centenary Annual Meeting at the
Royal Albert Hall, with the Princess Royal and
the Countess of Wessex in attendance.

W EDUCATION

Chapter 3

The education of countrywomen is enshrined in the WI constitution, drawn up in 1919. It defined the movement's main objectives as 'enabling women to take an effective part in rural life and development' and empowered the National Federation 'to make provision for the fuller education of countrywomen in citizenship, in public questions both national and international', and also for education in music, drama, and other cultural pursuits, and in agriculture, crafts, house-husbandry, and health.

Lady Denman, the NFWI's first chairman, had firm ambitions for the new organisation, which would not limit itself to food production and rural crafts but would free women from their previously rather narrow lives by offering them the chance to broaden their horizons and take much more active roles in their communities. An immediate focus was on showing women how to run meetings properly, not just so that their own WI meetings would have structure and coherence, but also so that women elected to public office would know what to expect and how to take a full and effective part. Now that women had been enfranchised, the WI was also anxious to ensure that they knew how to exercise their votes properly, and so laid on lectures on citizenship and civic affairs.

The standard format of a WI meeting was a half-hour talk on a topic such as infant welfare or travel abroad, followed by a practical demonstration. A lecture given in the 1920s to Orford (Suffolk) WI on women's duties as citizens, for example, was followed by a demonstration on how to bandage varicose veins. Many of the talks were educational in content, whether aimed simply at helping women to become better housewives and mothers or by encouraging them to venture into new, perhaps cultural, activities. And many of them led, as programmes developed and the WI increasingly found its feet, to full-blown, professionally taught courses on specific topics, often in alliance with local education authorities.

Denman College.
A student working on a fabric collage in the Design in Everyday Things course, 1964.

Bacon curing class.
Stonehall WI members being instructed in how to butcher, prepare, and salt pork in Lady Denman's kitchen, Balcombe Place, Balcombe, East Sussex, 1930s.

The lust for learning among countrywomen came as rather a surprise to some education authorities, who found themselves overwhelmed by the demand for their courses and in need of improving their provision. Through the agency of the WI, classes in a wide variety of subjects began to be offered in rural areas. WI members were elected to county education committees, and their educational needs were communicated to every level of government. A 1926 Board of Education report specifically commended the WI for the results of their efforts, which 'can only be regarded as phenomenal'.

The role of women in agriculture was always important; but there was little provision for providing them with practical education in that area. As a result of pressure by the NFWI, the government set up a committee to consider this deficiency, and invited Lady Denman to chair it. Her report, published in 1928, called for better provision for the agricultural education of women and for instruction aimed at areas of specific interest to them, horticulture for example, and farm household management. It also recommended the establishment of a college for women covering precisely those areas. Unfortunately, many of the report's ideas never came to fruition, mostly because of the looming Second World War.

Cultural pursuits too were encouraged and catered for. The inter-war period saw a surge of interest in music and drama within the WI. Villages organised elaborate pageants which often involved every man, woman, and child in the place, and some areas set up ambitious drama festivals where individual WIs put on performances which were evaluated by adjudicators. Many WIs formed choirs who sang at regional music festivals. Lewes (Sussex) WI for many years ran a festival that grew from a day-long event in 1921 to one lasting a full six days in 1933. It was open to all comers, and became highly prestigious, attracting choirs and bands from all over the county and also from many schools. Its repute was such that local authorities counted attendance at it by schools as part of their education, and it attracted musical adjudicators of high calibre like Adrian Boult and Malcolm Sargent.

Denman

The idea of establishing the Women's Institute's own college for adult education found fruitful soil in which to grow after the Second World War, when national educational policy was completely transformed and new initiatives found sympathetic ears. In 1946, driven on by Elizabeth Brunner, who was later to chair the NFWI, an appeal was launched to raise £60,000 to buy premises for a new college. They found the ideal house, Marcham Park in Oxfordshire, which had been used by the RAF during the war and was now up for sale. It was a fine Georgian house set in 100 acres with a walled kitchen garden and two cottages, and they bought it for £16,000. Two years later it opened as Denman College, named for the WI's first chairman who was present at the opening ceremony. It is now known simply as Denman.

The County Federations helped to furnish and equip the new college, and they still sponsor and look after all the residential rooms, which therefore each have their own unique feel. There is now a dedicated cookery school in a

Elizabeth Brunner, 1945.
The driving force behind the appeal to raise funds to help establish Denman College in September 1948.

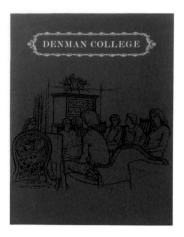

Souvenir booklet.
Denman College and its
activities, 1960s.

purpose-built facility in the grounds, beautifully equipped
and running a wide variety of courses – from the cuisine of
Italy, for example, to knife skills. Craft courses cover every
conceivable art and craft speciality, designed for students at
every level from beginners to the most experienced. Lifestyle
courses cover literature, history, music, tai chi, and handbell
ringing, among many others. The current catalogue lists well
over 600 options, some lasting an evening or a day, others
residential over a weekend or a few days.

For its first students – initially around 1,500 a year –
Denman offered a broadening of their horizons that many of
them could never have dreamed of experiencing, including
sometimes their first ever stay away from home. It is now
open to all comers, men and women both, though WI
members get a discount on the course fees. Its success over the
sixty-seven years of its existence is a tribute to the vision of its
founders; and the fact that it continues to flourish in the
twenty-first century indicates that there is still a strong need
and much enthusiasm for what it offers.

Educational outreach

Already in the 1920s, WIs were reaching out to their local
schools by encouraging them to join in music and drama
festivals. Today, individual WIs often liaise with schools by
offering opportunities to join in cooking and gardening
activities, and generally encouraging young women to
develop household skills, while the NFWI keeps up the
pressure on educational authorities to ensure that
schoolchildren are taught to cook and instructed in food
hygiene and avoiding wastage.

A rather more startling educational initiative is the
establishment of the first WI in a women's prison. Bronzefield
WI in HMP Bronzefield in Surrey was established in 2012 to
provide inspiration and opportunities to help members return
to normal life on their release. Bronzefield was purpose-built
for women prisoners and is the largest such institution in

Europe, housing category A and lower grade offenders as well as those on remand. Its WI is open to women who are on pre-release resettlement programmes and to the prison staff. It includes a book club, and has regular meetings run on the same principles as all WI groups; craft skills and cookery are in particular demand. Members range in age from the early twenties to the late sixties and, says its organiser, revel in the opportunity to forget they are in prison, learn new skills, join in activities, and generally acquire confidence in their ability to cope once they are back in the outside world. They have hosted coffee mornings for women who are members of WIs local to the prison, and will, says one of the national membership officers, be welcome in their own local WIs when they are released.

The WI in prison.
The banner of HMP Bronzefield WI, Surrey, one of the largest women's prisons in Europe, at a WI conference in 2013.

Denman College local
history course visit to
Abingdon, 1955.

'...to make provision for the fuller education of countrywomen'

– The Women's Institute Constitution 1919

A model of the future Denman College.
Made by secondary school children in Abingdon, seen here publicising the college at an
exhibition in Norfolk. The model shows the main house, H-shaped huts left by the RAF
– which later became Home Acres – and a walled garden with greenhouses. *c.*1948.

Denman College opening day.
Left: Sir Richard Livingstone, President of Corpus Christi College, Oxford, who formally opened Denman College. Seated, left to right, are guests of honour Gertrude Denman and Elizabeth Brunner. *Above*: Crowds gathering outside the main house following its opening, September 24 1948.

A rug for Denman College.
Members of Cumberland WI,
on opening day, with the rug
they made for the college
incorporating the WI 'For
Home and Country' badge.

Denman College staff.
Original staff members seated beside the lake in the college grounds, 1949. The first warden, Betty Christmas, and her pet labrador Sam are on the right.

Welcoming a new student.

A set of pictures shot for a 1960s Denman College souvenir booklet. The original caption reads: 'A lot of preparation and organisation has to be done before a member can lock her front door [*opposite above left*] and make her way – perhaps rather apprehensively – to the college. Once arrived the warm welcome of the warden [*opposite above right*] and her staff, and the sight of so many fellow members, soon make her feel at home. She is shown to her room which may be shared with others as in the Welsh bedroom [*opposite below*] or may be a single room in the New Croft. From that moment onwards the stresses and strains of leaving house and family will be forgotten in the absorbing interest of the course she has chosen. Time is short but when it comes to telling her Institute all about her few days at Denman College – and answering questions – the meeting may well continue outside the village hall [*above*]'.

Student life at Denman.

For many women, a stay at Denman College
was not just an opportunity to broaden their
knowledge and skills, but also a chance to meet
other like-minded women and enjoy evenings
of dance and chat in the Common Room.

Tea break.
Betty Christmas, warden, serving tea in the Denman College hall during a break in the 'Husbands and Wives' course, *c.*1955.

Needle and thread.

Left: Staff and students hold patchwork bedspreads made
for the college bedrooms by Women's Institute members,
1950s. *Above*: A student on the sewing course, *c*.1965.

Instruction.

Above: Mrs K Whitbourn from Sevenoaks, Kent, working on a bowl under the guidance of Donald Potter, 1955. *Below*: Thelma Jones demonstrating how to cut up chops to a group of students, 1940s. *Right*: A student practising wallpaper hanging under the watchful eye of an instructor, while other students take notes, 1970s.

Performance.
Left: Demonstrating different ways to curtsey at a drama rehearsal at Denman College, *c.*1960.
Below: A harp playing course at Denman, *c.*2000.

Art and language.
Above: Two students on an art course painting the scene across the lake, 1950s. *Left*: Calligraphy course, *c.*2000. *Right*: A Russian lesson, 1955.

Food preparation.
Left: Students preparing
vegetables in the Home
Acres kitchen, 1952.
Above: Preparing fruit
in the new cookery
school, 2014.

Taster day.
A watercolour class during a Denman 'taster day', 2007. 'The Country Wife', a wall hanging made by the WI for the Festival of Britain on London's South Bank in 1951, can be seen in the background.

PRIVATE PURSUITS

Chapter 4

Whatever its national image is, however big a splash its campaigns make in the media, the WI is essentially a federation of individual groups, each with its own identity, its own focus, its own priorities. The heart of the organisation lies in the WIs – numbering just under 7,000 – spread across England, Wales, and the islands, and the women who make up their membership. They are all part of the overarching National Federation and of their local County Federations, and they all send delegates to the Annual Meeting and lend their powerful voices to mandates and campaigns. And at a local level, their members engage in the activities that suit them as individuals and as part of their own unique WI.

It is a truism that the Women's Institutes all over England and Wales are known for making jam. And yes, they do! In both of the twentieth century's European wars, their jam making was an essential part of conserving the nation's produce and feeding the people. But it is also a major part of peacetime activities. In recent years, the WI's cookery school in the grounds of Denman has hosted a 'real jam' festival combined with a Christmas fair. Hundreds of jam makers compete for valuable prizes in a number of classes, including some specifically for men and children; one class is a WI set recipe, which in 2013 was a plum and mulled wine jam, and there is an overall winner in addition to all the class winners. The festival also includes cookery demonstrations and talks, a craft fair, a Christmas market, and Santa's grotto. Winners of *The Great British Bake Off* were among the demonstrators in 2013 (there was no festival in 2014 in view of the plans for the 2015 centenary).

Cakes are also a WI staple, and once again the awesome reputation of WI members is recognised in cookery competitions like the BBC's *Masterchef*, which often challenges its finalists to bake cakes for a formidable audience of WI grandees.

It goes almost without saying that good food and the

Backyard basketry.
Miss Brock of Essex making baskets, mats, and other receptacles from rushes which she gathered herself, 1942.

Women's Institute are synonymous. Cookery of all sorts is a focus for every individual Institute, both through talks and demonstrations from visiting speakers and through the efforts of the members; and the WI centrally runs a variety of courses within the Federations and at the cookery school at Denman. Recipes are published in *WI Life*, there is an impressive range of WI cookery books available for purchase, and for the 2015 centenary there is a special publication bringing together 100 recipes from the WI's extensive archives, spanning the decades and each set within its individual historical context.

It wouldn't be the Women's Institute, however, if campaigning for better nutrition was not part of its remit. The growing awareness of the dangers of childhood and adult obesity has led to initiatives such as Let's Cook Local, which ran from 2011 to 2013 and involved WI members supporting families in their areas by running basic cookery courses using local food, and teaching them to eat healthily and avoid waste. In some areas these courses are still being run, as part of the WI's constant aim to promote sustainability, food hygiene, and a better diet for everyone.

The WIs have also always been green-fingered, growing flowers, fruit, and vegetables for their own homes, for competitive shows, and for sale on their market stalls. Bacton and District (Suffolk East) WI kept an 'Operation Produce' logbook in 1948 (*see pages 155–7*), with hand-drawn illustrations, poems on the theme of 'Ode to a Potato', features titled 'News from the Sties' and 'Ch-Ch-Chickens', and testimonials to 'Those Who Have Dug' and 'Those Who Have Planted'.

Crafts too are a core WI focus. An analysis by Anne Stamper, Denman tutor, and Charlotte Dew of the subjects covered at WI meetings in the inter-war years shows a heavy emphasis on crafts of all sorts. Perhaps surprisingly, subjects like knitting and needlework did not form the largest percentage of the instruction on offer; WI members may already have been proficient enough in those activities.

Celebrity chef.
The Great British Bake Off's Paul Hollywood at a cookery demonstration, Real Jam Festival, Denman, 2012.

Rather, they focused on skills like toy making, skin curing, glove making, and – the largest category of all – basketry. They also sought training in what might previously have been considered men's work, for example cobbling, chair caning, tinkering, even plumbing.

Learning new craft skills to a high level led in many cases to the development of small, rural, profit-making industries, some of which gave women a degree of financial independence. The NFWI encouraged and supported this development, employing a professional to organise and oversee the burgeoning small businesses. They bulk-bought the raw materials and sold them through WI outlets. And in order to maintain high standards, they set up a Guild of Learners, whose aim was to revitalise dying country crafts, set standards, and train instructors. This focus remains central to WI activities today. The members of the Whiston Afternoon (Yorkshire South) WI were part of a local initiative to restore the village's manorial barn, and made three glorious wall hangings depicting local life to enhance its interior, along with a Millennium panel.

The material held in Federation archives contains rich memories of drama, music, and dance events put on by the Institutes, often with every member of every family in a village taking part in some way. In 1922 the Lancashire Federation was the first ever women's organisation to be allowed to take part in the Preston Guild Procession, an event that is held every twenty years to celebrate the history of the guilds in Preston and is thought to be the only celebration of its kind in England. They still take part, most recently in 2012.

Tennis, swimming, croquet, even cricket (c.1935) join with perhaps more niche activities like shooting, archery, gliding, and snooker among the panoply of sports and games with which WI members have engaged down the decades. There are national competitions in some of these activities, though more of them are local enthusiasms. The NFWI triathlon, of which the Wiltshire leg was won by

The Whiston wall hangings.
The centre panel of the three Whiston wall hangings, made for the village's restored manorial barn by the local WI's Craft Group in 1990.

Women's whites.
Members of the Weston Turville Women's Institute cricket team, *c.*1935.

Dilton Marsh WI (*see page 35*), challenged participants to cycle twenty miles, swim five miles, and walk or run fifty miles. All the Dilton Marsh members took part to some degree, with those of more limited mobility managing twenty yards each at a party in the president's garden.

Local campaigns too form part of the WI mix. In the 1940s and 1950s the Northamptonshire Federation took part in a project to design cottages for rural workers; the winning design was actually built in a village in the county. They also embarked on an initiative aimed at helping families in displaced persons' camps in Germany. A churchyard survey carried out by members of the Rushmere Evening (Suffolk East) WI is now a constant source of information for those researching family history. And both Suffolk Federations joined in partnership with the local authorities as part of the Millennium Challenge Landscape Audit to survey areas of the countryside for local planning departments.

More intimately, Wiltshire started a 'Skip to the Loo' campaign aimed at setting a minimum distance between the door and the toilet bowl in ladies' loos, which attracted international attention. And a locally focused campaign was waged by the members of the Middleton-cum-Fordley (Suffolk East) WI in order to impose a twenty miles per hour

'SKIP TO THE LOO'

THE REPORT OF A SURVEY OF LADIES PUBLIC LAVATORIES

by The Wiltshire Federation of Women's Institutes

£1.50

Ladies' convenience.
Wiltshire FWI's campaign report of a survey of ladies' public lavatories, 1997.

Restricting the rat run. Middleton-cum-Fordley's WI successfully campaigned to impose a 20 mph speed limit through their village in 2009.

speed limit within their small, rural village, which had previously been used as a rat run by heavy goods vehicles and commercial traffic. As Irene Ralph, who was the main organiser, reports, 'In 2009, as our WI approached its ninetieth birthday, we decided that in addition to the usual celebrations we wanted to give something lasting to our community. What better way than to campaign for a much needed twenty mph speed limit through the entire village? We have a primary school, a popular pub, a farm shop, children playing, and elderly residents, all wishing to enjoy a slower pace of life without constant danger from speeding traffic. So, with the support of our parish and county councils – we were the pilot scheme within Suffolk for the reduced speed limit – we carried out door-to-door petitions and also designed forms suitable for visitors to the village. We received overwhelming support and – three and a half years later, with some compromise along the way – we finally saw the twenty mph signs installed.'

Among the most beautiful records of local work carried out by the Institutes is the *Dorset Federation of Women's Institutes War Record 1939–1945*. This is a large, leather-bound, mostly hand-written, gorgeously designed account of the war work done by each of the Institutes in the county (*see pages 66–7*). It was one of five books designated as a unique 'hidden treasure' by the British Library in 2007. It is only one part of a vast archive of material held by Women's Institute branches all over the country recording and celebrating the huge swathe of work and fun with which its members have engaged during the first century of its existence.

A WI meeting, 1953.

'...to do our utmost
to make our village
the centre of good in
our neighbourhood'

– Llanfairpwll WI

Welcoming a new member.

Left: Her application having been accepted, a new member of Flamstead WI is
handed her membership card by the president and is applauded by fellow members.
Above: She knocks on the door of an older member who greets her and her baby.
Below: She talks with her new friends at the Hertfordshire FWI produce show, *c*.1947.

Outside the meeting.
At the monthy meeting
of Burstow WI, 'the
president reminds
another member of a
promise', 1950s.

Butchery and baking.

Above left: Miss Rhys pointing to 'Ferdinand the Bull' which, along with pictures of a pig and lamb, she used for talks on different cuts of meat, *c.*1957.

Above: A talk on baking, Queen Mary Hall, London, 1957.

A handicraft exhibition.
Opposite: Edith Hamilton, wearing her craft badge and watched by her sister Gertrude, embroidering a quilted linen handkerchief case to be presented to Princess Elizabeth for Princess Margaret Rose. *Below*: Queen Elizabeth watches a Women's Institute member demonstrating chair caning on a chair to be presented to Princess Elizabeth. *Right*: The poster for the exhibition, 1938.

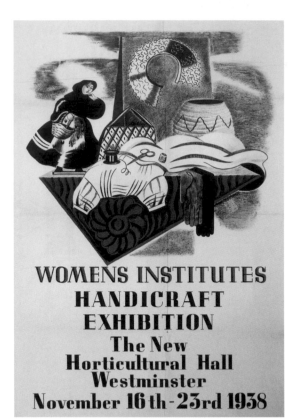

Country produce.

A Women's Institute flower and produce
stall in Saffron Walden, Essex, 1940s.

Street stalls.
Above: WI produce
stall selling flowers,
preserves, and vegetables
at Cirencester, 1933.
Left: WI members selling
cabbages at Storrington
outdoor market, 1944.

A Christmas market.

Above: Queuing to be served by Henley WI. The blackboard reads, 'A happy Xmas to all our helpers and customers' and 'Holly wreathes 6/6 each', while the counter (*right*) groans under the weight of fruit, vegetables, preserves, and a wild rabbit, *c.*1935.

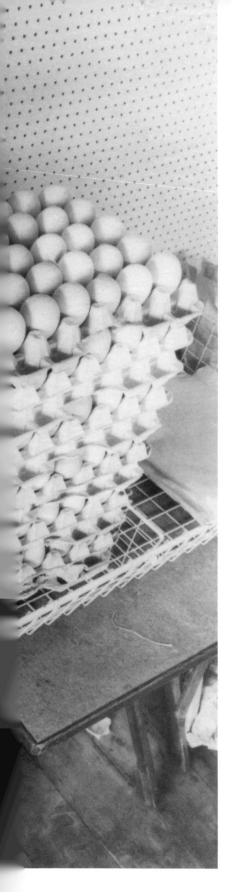

Open for business.
Left: Behind the counter at a
WI market stall with accounts
register and cash bowl, *c.*1950.
Above: WI poster, 1945.

Operation Produce.

Left: Agricultural student Judy Humberstone picking pears for the canning club of the Women's Institute at Ashton-under-Edge in the Vale of Evesham, of which her mother was president, 1948.

Right and following pages: A few pages from Bacton WI's wittily illustrated Log Book of 'Operation Produce', 1948.

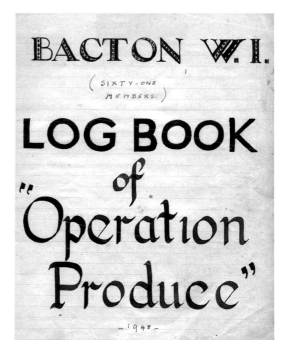

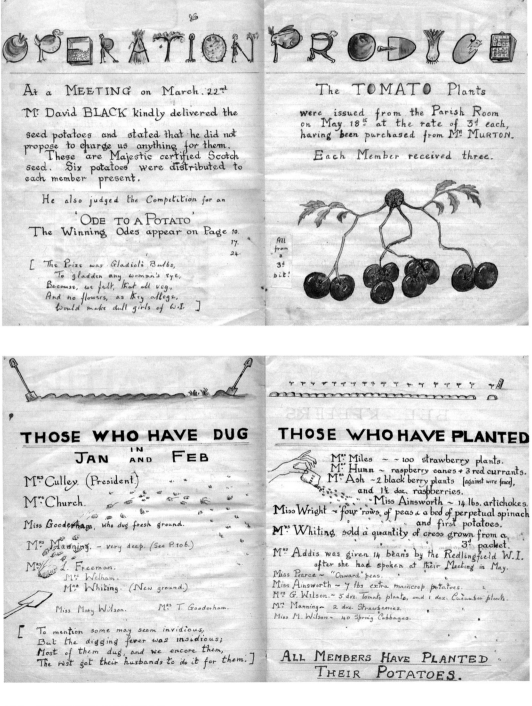

OPERATION PRODYCE

At a MEETING on March. 22nd

Mr David BLACK kindly delivered the seed potatoes and stated that he did not propose to charge us anything for them.

These are Majestic certified Scotch seed. Six potatoes were distributed to each member present.

He also judged the Competition for an 'ODE TO A POTATO'

The Winning Odes appear on Page 10.
17.
24.

[The Prize was Gladioli Bulbs,
  To gladden any woman's eye,
  Because, we felt, that all veg,
  And no flowers, as they allege,
  Would make dull girls of W.I.]

The TOMATO Plants

were issued from the Parish Room on May 18th at the rate of 3d each, having been purchased from Mr MURTON.

Each Member received three.

All from a 3d bit!

THOSE WHO HAVE DUG
IN JAN AND FEB

Mrs Culley. (President.)

Mrs Church.

Miss Gooderham, who dug fresh ground.

Mrs Manning. - very deep. (See P.106.)

Mrs L. Freeman.
Mrs Welham.
Mrs Whiting. (New ground.)

Miss Mary Wilson.   Mrs T. Gooderham.

[To mention some may seem invidious,
  But the digging fever was insidious;
  Most of them dug, and we encore them,
  The rest got their husbands to do it for them.]

THOSE WHO HAVE PLANTED

Mr Miles ~ ~ 100 strawberry plants.
Mr Humm ~ raspberry canes + 3 red currants.
Mr Ash ~ 2 black berry plants [against wire fence],
and 1½ doz. raspberries.
~ Miss Ainsworth ~ 14 lbs. artichokes.
Miss Wright ~ four rows of peas & a bed of perpetual spinach
and first potatoes.
Mrs Whiting sold a quantity of cress grown from a
3d packet.
Mrs Addis was given 14 beans by the Redlingfield W.I.
after she had spoken at their Meeting in May.
Miss Pearce ~ "Onward" peas.
Miss Ainsworth ~ 7 lbs extra maincrop potatoes.
Mrs G. Wilson ~ 5 doz. Tomato plants, and 1 doz. Cucumber plants.
Mrs Manning ~ 2 doz. Strawberries.
Miss M. Wilson ~ 40 Spring Cabbages.

ALL MEMBERS HAVE PLANTED THEIR POTATOES.

NEWS FROM THE STIES

Miss Gooderham is fattening two pigs on household refuse.

Mrs. T. Gooderham is attempting to fatten a pig but it has grown, not only in girth, but also in charm, and has become a Pet..............

Mrs. Welham has been fattening a pig — Killed in October.

Mrs. Jackson has been feeding pigs.

Mrs. Ash is fattening one pig, which is allocated for Christmas consumption; and six others to be sold when they are too fat for their stye.

DON'T FORGET!
We've contributed to the PROGRESS REPORT on Page 15.

Ch-Ch-Chickens.

Mrs. Ash hatched 12 Chickens.

Mrs. Webb has raised 4 Pullets, and 3 Cockerels.

Nurse Woodward is rearing 11 Chickens. (and ate the Cockerels in the Autumn.)

Mrs. Elmer is rearing 40 Pullets.
Mrs. J. Betts helped to rear day-old Chicks.
Mr. G. Wilson reared 50 Chickens (all Pullets.) 12 Ducks.
Mrs. Welham hatched 125 Ducks & 25 Turkeys.
Miss Pearce has helped to look after 40 Poultry.

Mrs. Forsdyke hatched 18 Chicks, 5 Cockerels.

Mrs. Jackson hatched 2 doz. Chickens.

Mrs. Cadley hatched a sitting: 5 Cockerels, 4 Pullets.

The 'HOME-CAN'

Purchased Jointly by 3 MEMBERS.

Results: Mrs. Ash.
7 Tins Plums
3 Tins Blackberries
3 Tins Beans
7 Tins Pears.

Mesdames Addis-Meadows.

5 2lb. Tins of Pears.
Later: 6 2lb. Tins of Pears.

Miss Ainsworth.

9 Tins of Tomatoes.

Just for fun.

Above: A paper hat competition
being judged by the Duke of
Bedford and Johnny Dartmouth,
1964. *Right*: Lexden WI members
in a competiton to eat jelly
with knitting needles, 1959.

Dancing.

Left: Members of Eastgate Women's Institute practising country dancing to a gramophone in the fields of Weardale, County Durham, 1953. *Above*: Dancing round a maypole at a rehearsal for the Oxfordshire FWI pageant, 1960s.

Parading the banner.

Above left: Four Kemsing WI members in a
procession through Maidstone with a banner
depicting the craft of jam-making, *c*.1920.
Above: A parade of banners at the Buckinghamshire
FWI Rally, Hampden House, June 1947.

"The Laughing Mind" Performed for County Drama Festival
West Malling W.I. 1934

Plays and pageants.
Above left: West Malling WI performing at the Kent County Drama Festival, 1934. *Above right*: Members of an unidentified Women's Institute dressed in medieval costume at an outdoor pageant, 1927. *Left*: Members of Brackley WI in costume as a giant suit of cards. The ace bears the local WI's crest. 1915. *Right*: Norah Gibbs as 'Miranda' (with 'Ferdinand') at Warwickshire FWI's pageant, 1930s.

A dramatic interpretation. Members of the Warwickshire FWI performing the Clock Minuet in Georgian costume, 1930s.

All together now.

Above: A recorder class at Suffolk East FWI headquarters in Ipswich, 1950s. *Right above*: Members of a Women's Institute choir singing at The Grove, Consett, County Durham at the time of the Queen's coronation, June 1953. *Right below*: Members of West Kent FWI hand bell ringing at their county music festival, 1974.

The wife of a crusader, 1250. Costume made by Buckinghamshire FWI. The Royal Albert Hall, 1969.

The Brilliant and the Dark

The influence of the Women's Institute continues to be far-reaching, and is often to be found in unusual places. In the late 1960s, the National Federation commissioned a ground-breaking piece of music from Malcolm Williamson, with Ursula Vaughan Williams as librettist, called *The Brilliant and the Dark*. It followed women's lives down the centuries from the Middle Ages to the Second World War, seeing contemporary events through characters such as witch hunters, plague victims, crusaders' wives, embroiderers, and war workers. It was performed four times at the Royal Albert Hall in 1969 by a choir of 1,000 female amateur singers.

The Wars of the Roses, 1445–1485. Costumes made by WI members from Worcestershire and West Kent.

In 2010, with permission, the work was radically reworked for a twenty-four-strong group of women singers called Gaggle, who used elements of the original but also brought it up to date with references to 'honour' killings, military rape in Africa, and female genital mutilation. The group intend to keep updating it, keep telling the history of women through song, allowing it to grow and evolve and to be part of an unending musical process that allows women to tell their own stories in their own voices. Once again, it was the WI who set in motion an initiative with continued modern resonance.

Witch hunters, 1612.

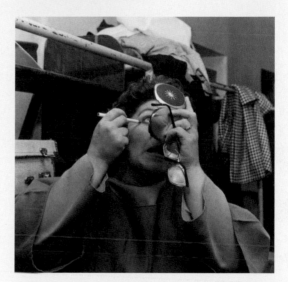

The cast, mostly amateur, ready themselves backstage for a performance of *The Brilliant and the Dark* at the Royal Albert Hall, 1969. The cast of 1,300 WI members – consisting of 49 choirs, 8 pianists, 8 soloists, 120 actors and 30 dancers – were chosen at county and regional festivals.

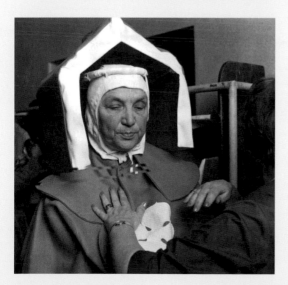

Singing for Joy.
Centenary Choir
participants the
Surrey Serenaders
competing in the
Dorking heat of
Singing for Joy, 2014.

The competitive spirit.

Above left: Contestants in the Little Black Dress ethical fashion competition at the Fashion and Textile Museum, London, 2011.
Above right: A three-legged race during Avon FWI's Olympic Torch celebrations, 2012.

A variety of sports.

Left: Two finalists at the NFWI/Milk Marketing Board Tennis Championship, 1985. *Right*: Gabrielle Goodall, Press Correspondent of Steyning Downland (West Sussex) WI, (and Secretary of the British Women's Pistol Association), firing a 22 bore Browning 150 Match, 1973. *Below*: Sheila Hawkins Clophill from the Bedfordshire FWI takes aim, 1982.

Flying high.
Patricia Ridger,
treasurer of Ludford
WI, Lincolnshire
North FWI, in her
LS4 single-seat
glider, 2013.

TODAY AND TOMORROW

Coda

In 1975, when the Women's Institute celebrated its diamond jubilee, Lady Anglesey (chairman 1966–9) summed up its achievements: 'For sixty years we have been outspoken but also moderate; today the pressures are stronger to act emotionally and sectionally and to move towards extremes. These pressures will be on us too. Tolerant and informed we must continue to be, apathetic we must not become, but our spread, geographically and socially through a considerable cross-section of society, gives us a special opportunity – to be passionate for moderation, to hang on to rational argument and common sense, and to work for the good of the whole community. It will require strenuous activity and may not be at all easy. Let us make sure that by the time we reach our centenary our members still enjoy the same opportunity for freedom of expression.'

Now, in the centenary year, it is clear that Lady Anglesey's hopes for the future have been achieved. The WI is stronger than ever, but there have inevitably been changes.

When it started, the WI was an entirely rural affair, focusing on countrywomen. It dealt with rural matters and found its strength in underpinning country skills and ways of life. Yet its foundation coincided with the women's suffrage movement, and its founders were formidable women in their own right. So the new Women's Institute quickly established a female-based ethos which insisted on democracy and independence. Making the views of its members known, and highlighting issues that mattered to them, soon became a vital part of its activities, while its educational and community aims also remained central. Its strength and its focus, clearly established right at the beginning, sustained it during many decades of wartime, society upheaval, the development of technologies that changed the world, and the growth of the sort of global community that its founders could never have imagined.

That original ethos remains unchanged. Today the WI is governed by a Board of Trustees made up of WI members

Past, present, and future. A wartime Christmas experience was recreated by the Cambridge Blue Belles WI at their Home Front party in 2013, where they enjoyed authentic 1940s cooking and learned the Lindy Hop.

voted for by the membership, with a chair at its head and a series of sub-committees. The NFWI – which is defined as covering England, Wales, Jersey, Guernsey, and the Isle of Man – has an office in London which is the organisation's headquarters, and Denman has its own roster of staff. The constitution, which has been amended so that 'it now embraces the interests of women in both rural and urban communities', lays down clear rules about the operation of individual WIs, which are constituent members of their Federations, which are members of the National Federation. It states that 'All women who are interested in the values and purposes of the WI may join, no matter what their views on religion or politics may be,' and that 'WIs are charitable and everything they do must be consistent with that special legal status'.

Each WI, the rules state, must meet at least eleven times a year, and hold a formal Annual Meeting at which the officers are elected: a president, up to three vice-presidents, a secretary, and a treasurer.

So far, so formal, as the WI has been from the start. But the change to the constitution which welcomed urban WIs alongside rural is only part of the change in the way it operates today. During the final decades of the twentieth century, it is fair to say that the movement was facing a crisis. Its membership was declining fast in the face of an increasingly consumerist society which saw its values as old-fashioned and out of touch with the modern world.

By the end of the century membership was at an all-time low. But several high-profile news items began to slow, and then reverse, the decline. The handbagging of Tony Blair; the Calendar Girls; the appearances on *Masterchef*; the widely reported campaign against excess packaging and other key campaigning action – all started to persuade the public and the media to question the traditional image of the WI. Perhaps its members were not so fuddy duddy after all.

Fifteen years after Tony Blair so disastrously misjudged his

WI audience, membership is growing rapidly, with many
more WIs being established in towns and cities, and its
recruits coming from a much wider, younger, ethnically
diverse, and urban demographic. The huge success of *The
Great British Bake Off* and its spin-offs like the *Great British
Sewing Bee* has led to a surge in the desire to take up
traditional crafts and skills. Many of the women who join
today do so because the WI offers precisely those traditional
values and opportunities that are regarded as increasingly
desirable. But others also see it as a warm, welcoming
community in what can sometimes be an isolating and lonely
society, and one which offers them a forum within which they
can express their altruism and their social conscience. And
one with jam and cake as part of the mix.

The women of 1915 would perhaps look with astonishment
– and envy – at what the women of today enjoy in terms of
freedom to work in any profession they wish, to plan their
families, to make their own decisions about their lives. They
might also look with pity at the stresses of modern life and
the increased strain on women who are urged to 'have it all'.
But they would be able to contemplate the WI and recognise
what they see: a movement that retains the same values and
promotes the same virtues as the one they set up a century
ago; but also one that embraces all the freedoms and
advantages of modern womanhood while continuing to fight
and work for change and improvement, and to remain hugely
important and relevant in today's world.

Following pages:
Members of the East End
WI in London decorating a
church hall, 2008.

List of subscribers

Valerie Aaron
Aberedw WI
Ginny Addison-
  Smith
B Adlam
Sarah-Jane Ainley
Chris Ainsworth
Shirley Aiton
Wendy E Aldous
Jean Alker
Judith Allen
Karen Allen
Valerie Allworthy
Geraldine Ames
Judith Anderson
Vicki Anderson
Lynne Andrews
Mary Andrews
Lillian Angell
Diane Appleby
Vanessa Archer
Joyce Armer
Margaret Armitage
Jill Armsby
Gail J Armstrong
Armthorpe WI
Jacqueline Arnold
Arnside and Arnside
  Knott WI
Jeanette
  Arrowsmith
Janet M Ashcroft
Tricia Ashdown
Ashurst WI
Julie Aston-Vize
Gwen Attle
Norma Austin
Diana Axtell
Jane Ayres
Jennifer A Babb
Norma Baggs
BJ Ingrid Bailey
JM Bainbridge
Jackie Baines
Ann Sheila Baker
Jill Baker
Julia Baker
Marian Baker
Maureen Baker
Margaret Baldini
Carroll Baldwin
Isabel Baldwin
Anne Ball
Judith Ball
Jean Banks
Sarah Banks
Ann Barber
Elizabeth Ann
  Barber
Bardsey-cum-Rigton
  WI
Barbara Ann Barker
Christine Elaine
  Barker
Imelda Barker
Monica Barker
Diane Barlow
AC Barnes
Anne Barnes
Veronica Barnes
Pat Barnett
Avril V Barratt
Barbara Barrett

Barrow-upon-Trent
  WI
Pam Bartlett
Jacqueline Barugh
Freda Basley
Coral Batchelor
Sue Batchelor
Deborah Baudains
Judy Baxendale
Barbara
  Bayes-Crysell
June Bayles
Alison Beadle
Kate Beardmore
Mary Beasley
AJ Beattie
DM Becker
Yvonne Bee
Belan WI
Marion and Angela
  Bendy
Gillian Benfield
P Benn-Cross
Anne Bennett
Iris Bennett
Janice Bensley
Patricia Benstead
Bere Regis WI
Carole Mary Beretta
Diane Berry
Christine Best
Janis Bethel
Dianne Bevan
Iris Bex
Ann Beynon
Mary Bickerton
Doris M Bicknell
Bicknoller WI
JL Bignell
Binbrook and
  District WI
Mary Bingham
Fiona Birchall
Elizabeth A Bird
Hazel Bird
Jacqueline Bird
Phyllis Bird
Noreen Birnie
Rosemary Bishton
  MBE
Rosemary Black
Elma Blackmore
Margaret Blackwell
Anne Blagdon
Joan Bland
Mary Blathwayt
Ruth Blindell
Berenice Blurton
Anna Bold
GW Boldero
Beverley Bones
DJ Bonner
Margaret C Bonser
Bontfaen WI
Ruby Mary Booker
Kathleen Boothman
Barbara J Borrer
Bosherston WI
S Botham
Valerie Botting
Ann Bottomley
Bourne WI
Jeanette Bourne

Norma A Bowers
Ann Box
Mair Boyd
Lesley Boyden
Charlotte E Boyes
Karen R Boyes
Ann Boyle
Norma Bradley
Sheila Bradley
Jean Bramwell
Braunston WI
Linda Brazier
Sandra Breen
Joy Breslin
Margaret Ann
  Breyley
Angela Brice
Rebe Brick
Bridge (Holt) WI
Gina Brierley
Patricia Bright
Brislington WI
Broadbridge Heath
  WI
Pam Broadhead
Diana Broadhurst
Alison Brockliss
Carol Brodie
Stella Bromley
Virginia Bromley
Yvonne Brookfield
Deborah Brooks
Phyllis L Brooks
Anita Dawn Brough
Freda Brownell
Betty Brown
Carol M Brown
Dinah CM Brown
Evelyn M Brown
Marilyn Brown
Rita A Brown
Sandy Brown
Sharron Brown
Dr SM Brown
Susan Brown
Yvonne Brown
Barbara Rucastle
Janet Bryan
Buckinghamshire
  Federation of WIs
Leanne Buckley
Anne Bufton-
  McCoy
Bugbrooke WI
Marilyn Bull
Elizabeth A Bullas
Anne R Bullman
Bonny Bullock
Susan M Bunn
Maureen Bunnage
Bures WI
Sue Burgess
Burghclere and
  Newtown WI
Peggy Burgin
Nicole Burgum
Eileen Frances Burn
Burnham Copse WI
Teresa Burningham
Burstwick WI
Avril Burton
Donna Butcher
Sue Butcher

Vera Butterworth
Joy Button
Joyce Buxton
Liz Buxton
Bwlchllan WI
Gillian Bywater
Jean Cadin
Caerleon WI
Christine Caleya
  Chetty
Marie Caltieri
Judith Cameron
Mary Cane
SF Capewell
Glenys Care
Joss Carpreau
Jennifer Carter
Vera Carter
Muriel Cary
CE Case
Pamela Cash
Rosemary
  Castlehouse
M Cattermole
Annabelle Caughlin
Gill Cave
Joan Cawthorne
Chadwell-St-Mary
  WI
Valerie Chamberlain
Jeanette M
  Chambers
Lesley Chambers
Lisa Chambers
Olive Chapman
Margaret Anne
  Chappell
Prudence Chard
Therese M
  Charnock
Chedworth WI
Lally Cheeseman
Patricia Cheesman
Chelsfield
  Afternoon WI
Chew Stoke WI
Jean Child
Sheila May Childs
Cholsey WI
Pauline Church
Church Village WI
Ada Churchill
Churchstoke WI
Clare WI
Gillian Clark
Judith Clark
Kath Clarke
Mary Clarke
Claxton and Sand
  Hutton WI
Cleeve-by-Goring
  WI
Jackie Cleveland
Phyl Cliff
Margaret Clowes
Ruth Clowes
MC Cobb
Jenny Cobley
Cockfield WI
June P Cofield
Joyce Cole
Val Coleman
Barbara Collard

Yvonne Collard
Margaret Genia
  Collin
Katie Collins
Sophie Collins
Marion Colman
Comeytrowe and
  District WI
Anne Conchar
Maj-Britt Connett
Mary Connick
Beryl Conway
Christine Cook
Mary Cookson
Suzanne Cooling
Jill Cooper
Ros Cooper
Ann Corby
Susan Corfield
Shirley D Corke
Margaret Cornock
Karen Cotterill
Cottingham Green
  WI
Gill Cotton
Jane Couch
Joyce Coulling
Jean Couture
Vivien Cove
Coverdale WI
Dorothy Anne
  Cowans
Barbara Cowburn
Dyllis Cowen
Barbara Cox
Julia Cox
Margaret Cox
Muriel Cox
Mary Crane
Freda Anne
  Crawforth
Margaret Creek
Creigiau WI
Maureen Crew
Annie Elizabeth
  Crick
Miora Cridland
Sharon Cripps
Linda Crispin-
  Kilworth
Marlene M
  Critchlow
Cromer WI
Crookham Village
  WI
Cross Inn WI
Crowborough St
  Johns WI
Peggy Crump
Kathy Crust
Viv Culley-Appley
Janet Cumner
Patricia N Curling
Kathryn Cuthbert
Katy-Jane Cuthbert
Maggie Dainton
Susan Dales
Ann Daniells
Jackie Daniels
Sandra Dare
Joanne Elizabeth
  Davey
Jane Davies-Sayer

Anne Davies
Felicity Davies
Gwyneth M Davies
Jill Davies
Liz Davies
Rosemarie Davies
Vicky Davies
Mary A Davis
Philippa M Davis
Elizabeth Davison
Janice Dawson
Carol Deakin
Norma Deane
Deeping St James
  WI
Stella Demery
Rosemary E Denly
Dorothy Dennison
Christine Denton
Olive Denyer
Dersingham Evening
  WI
Chris Devlin
KM Dickson
J Ditchfield
Hilary Dix
P Dix
Judy Dixon
Judith Domleo
Wendy Donovan
Margaret J Dooley
Jean Dorey
Mary Dorling
Patrice Dorling
Jo Dorrell
Mary Dorrell
Jane Doughty
Dorothy Douse
Sandra Maureen
  Downing
Nicola Drake
Marion Drinkwater
Elizabeth Duck
MJ Dudgeon-Smith
Sylvia Dudman
Holli Louise
  Duggan
Vicki Dumbleton
Vivien Dumbleton
Diana K Dunham
Chris Durrant
Durley Divas WI
Vivienne Durne
Heather Dyer
Jane Dyer
Gillian Dykes
Sheila A Eastwood
Eaton-By-Congleton
  WI
Lesley Eccles
Patricia Eden
Mary Edmunds
Anita Edwards
Hilary Edwards
Judith Edwards
Margaret Edwards
MD Eeles
Effingham WI
Egerton WI
Ann Elam
Eleth WI
Maralyn Elkin
Laura Elliott

Veronica Elliott
Avis Elliss
Gail Ellson
Elm Tree and
  Fairfield WI
Pauline Mary
  Elsome
Janet England
Erwood and District
  WI
Essendon WI
Euxton WI
Barbara Evans
Bronwyn Anne
  Evans
Jennifer Evans
Lesley Evans
Margaret Rose
  Evans
Pamela Everett
Rachel Everett
Helen Louise Everitt
Penelope Ezra
Joanne Dawn Falla
Molly Falla
Moreen Beatrice
  Fallon
Elsie Faragher
Raena Farley
Farlington WI
Stephanie Farren
  Brown
Jenny Farthing
Doris Faulkner
Gillian Faulkner
Lynne Faulkner
Marjorie A Faulkner
Jan Febery
Federation of Essex
  WIs
Zoe Fenwick
Beverley Ferey
Absolutely WI
  Ferndown
Barbara Ferris
Ferry Hill WI
Marion F Field
Sarah Field
June Fielden
Margaret Fields
Marilyne Findlow
Jeanette Fish
Barbara Fisher
Barbara C Fisher
Elizabeth Fisher
Margaret Fisher
Pamela Fisher
June Ann Fleetwood
Ann Fletcher
Lynn Flory
Patricia Anne Foard
Margaret Footner
Adele Ford
Ancia J Ford
Barbara Ford
Gillian Forrow
Jill R Forrow
Judith Forster
Rosemary Forsyth
Jean Forsythe
Mary Foster
Sheila E Foster
H Foxall

Christine Frame
Janet Francis
Liz Francis
Margaret E Francis
Carolyn Frank
Sue Frayling-Cork
Jennifer Friar
George T Frog
Una Froggatt
Christine Frost
S Frost
Russ Fry
Betty Furner
Marilyn Futter
Donna Galek
Eileen Gamble
Joy M Gammon
Carole Garland
Kath Garner
Garsington WI
Gladys Gascoigne
Greta Gaskell
Patricia D Geiger
Elizabeth Gentil
Anne George
Gillian M George
Pauline M George
Pamela Gerrard
Dinah Gibbons
Christine A Gifford
Betty Gilbert
Lynda Giles
Phillipa Giles
Rachel Gill
Hazel Gillingham
Pauline Gillman
Elizabeth Gingell Tracey Girdler-Rogers
Girsby WI
Rachel Anne Gissing
Ann Gleave
Julie Ann Glentworth
Gobowen WI
Hilary Godfrey
Mari Anne Goldsworthy
Julie Goodchild
Shirley Anne Goodman
Sally Goodrick
Pauline Goodwin
Phyllis Goodwin
Janet Gosling
Marion Gough
Laura Goulden
Megs Graham-Rack
Angela Graham
Val Graham
Chris Grainger
M Grant
Jean M Graves
Olwyn Gravestock
AM Gray
Priscilla Gray
Great Rollright WI
Great Torrington WI
Great Totham WI
Julia Green
Margaret Green
Sally Ann Green
Shirley Green
BA Greenhouse
Peggie Gregson
Rita Grehan

Linda Griesiell
Margaret C Griffin
June Griffiths
Beryl Griggs
Margaret Grindley
Jean Groom
Helen Groves
Margaret L Groves
Pamela Guerin
Rose Gugan
Guidepost and Sheepwash WI
Francesca Gunns
Christina Guthrie
Judith Haldenby
Kath Hales
Margaret M Hall
Marilyn Hall
Victoria Hall
Janet Hallett
Judith Hallimond
Ann Hallworth
Linda Charlotte Halstead
Marjorie Hambly
Rosemary Hamilton
Hammerwich WI
Jean Hammond
Doreen Hancock
Alison Handley
Evelyn Hankin
Alison Hannaford
Valerie Hansell
Harden And District WI
Glennis Hardman
Delia Hardy
Joyce Harkness
Harlestone WI
Vivienne Harlow
Pauline Harris
Sue Harris
Thelma Joyce Harris
Betty Harrison
Elizabeth Hart
Joy Hart
Jennifer Hartley
Karen K Hartley
Sandra Harvey
Susan Harvey
Tina Harvey
Val Harvey
Ann Haskins
Hatch Grange WI
Maureen Hatcher
Beth Hathaway
Penelope Iris Hawkins
Mavis Hawkyard
Barbara Haxby
Margaret E Hay
Kim Hayman
Avril Haynes
Jill Haynes
Karen Hayward
Carole Headland
Marion Heald
Helena Heald
Patricia G Heath
Sheila Heath
Christine Hebron
Carol Ann Henderson
Jacqueline Henderson
Margaret Herriot
Carol Ann Hewitt (née Rumney)

Pamela Hewitt
Jane Alexandra Hiatt
Julie Higgins
June Higgins
Rosemary Higgs
SM Higgs
High Legh WI
Highley WI
Highweek WI
Barbara Irene Hill
Jennifer Hill
May Hill
Stephanie Hill
Valerie J Hillier
Sheila Hinton
Carol Hird
Janet Hirst
Mary Hitchcock
Lorna Hoare
Hoby, Rotherby and Brooksby WI
Frances and Yolande Hocking
Maggie Hodges, daughter of Lottie Cope
Gill Hodgson
Dolly Hogan
Yvonne Hoggarth
Pauline Holbrook
Marilyn Holehouse
Dr Deirdre M Holes
Jean Holes
Tovah Hollingshead
Gloria Hollins
Janet Ada Holman
Pauline Holmes
Maureen Hooper
Lorna Hopper
Hordle WI
Horeston Grange WI
Pearl Horgan
Margaret Hornby
Susan Hornby
Jeanette Hortop
Valerie Hough
Betty Houghton
Wendy Kathrine Houghton
Kay Howard
Marjorie S Howden
Jan Howe
Rachel Anne Howe
BA Howitt
Rosemary Howland
Mary Howse
Doreen Hubbard
Vera Huckle
Heather M Hughes
Sheila M Hughes
Joyce Hundleby
Maureen Hunt
Eileen Hurd
Sharon Hurrell
Beverly P Hurst
Yvonne Huston
Penny Hutchings
Melody Hutchinson
Fiona Huxley
Sylvia Hyams
Thelma Hynes
Jenny Ingram-Cotton
Gina Ireland
Daphne Itter
Lesley Joan Jacklin

Christine Jackson
Joyce Jackson
Marilyn Jackson
Rowena Jackson
Tricia Jackson
Joyce James
Patricia James
Yvonne James
Marion Jeffery
Pamela Jeffery
Lesley Jeffries
Marilyn Jelfs
Gladys Jenkins
Lorna Jenkins
Linda Jenkinson
Patricia Jenner
Debbie Jessel
Rita Ann Jillings
MW John
Ann Johns
Ann C Johnson
Dorothy Johnson
Jill Johnson
Margaret H Johnson
Sheila Johnston
R Joisce
Elizabeth Jones-Griffiths
Barbara Ann Jones
C Jones
Christine Jones
Christine Matchwick Jones
Dawn Jones
Eileen Jones
Hilary Jones
Jean Huw Jones
Jennifer Jones
Jenny Jones
Lilian G Jones
Mair Jones
Rita Jones
Rose Jones
Sheila M Jones
Sheila Georgina Joynes
Judith Junor
Diana Justham
Angela Kane
Ann Keeley
Joan M Kelsey
Kay Kemp
Sue Kendall
Margaret Kennedy
Mary Kenny
Beryl Kettle
Barbara Killen
Sylvia Kilshaw
Hazel M King
Pam King
Maureen Kings
Kingswood Abbey WI
Margaret Kinley
Pauline Kirby
Sue Kirby
June Kirk
Margaret Kirk
Carole Kirkham
VA Kirkham
Kirton and Falkenham WI
Joan Klopke
Carolyn Knapman
Ann Knee-Robinson
Hazel Knight
Helen Knight

Maureen A Knight
Rosemary Joan Knight
Susan Knight
Jenny Knights
Knowbury WI
Joan L'Amie
Sarah Lain (in memory of Nanna)
Jennifer Lait
Carol Lamb
Betty Lambert
Enid Lambert
GM Lambert
Janet Lane
Janice Langley
E Lasbury
Sandra Law
Wendy Lawrence
Lawrenny and Martletwy WI
Anne Lawson
Linda Lawson
Anne Laxton
Maureen Le Feuvre
Gill Le Queux
Kate Le Queux
Susan Mary Leah
Gladys Lear
Christina Lee
Lynda Lee
Janet Lees
Sheilah Legg
Lin Lenox
Angela Lester
Lewes Neville WI
Betty M Lewis
Carol Lewis
Celia Lewis
Julia Natalie Lewis
Linda Lewis
Anne R Lindley
Sharon Lindley
Judith A Lindsay
Patricia Lindsay
Marilyn Lines
ME Lines
Jae Link
Pauline Littler
Llandysul WI
Llangwryfon WI
Llanhennock WI
Llannon WI
Llantilio Crossenny WI
Doreen Lloyd
MP Lloyd
Jo Locke
Denise Londesbrough
Jill London
Angela Long
Elizabeth Ellen Long
Mary Long
Susan Longbottom
Longlevens WI
Heather Jean Looney
Lovedean WI
Carole Lovell
Jean Lovett
Patricia M Lowe
Elizabeth Lowrey
Penelope Lucas
Annette Luckins
Mave Luff

Debbie Lumley
Lydbrook WI
Jean MacDougall
Joyce Mace
Frances MacKenzie
Nicola Mackey
Deborah MacLeod
Mary I Maddison
Magnolia WI
Irene Magor
Patricia Eileen Magowan
Sheila Mahoney
June Maidens
Deirdre Mair
June Maitland
Elizabeth Maloney
Elizabeth Mangle
Ruth Manley
J Mann
Christine Mansell
Deedy Mansfield
Rosemary Marles
Marlow Bottom WI
Pauline Marney
Lesley Marriage
Jacqueline Marsh
Penny Marsh
Ann Marshall
Pauline A Marshall
Olive Marston
Marston Green WI
Marion Martin
Dorothy Maskell MBE
Barbara Mason
Dorothy Massingham
Maggie Masters
Janet Matthews
Pat Matthews
Ann May
Helen Mayfield-Ella
Pat Maylor
Katherine McCallum
Ruth McCartney
Liz McDermott
Ruth McDougall
Linda McGowan
Jane McHale
Jess McKillop
Jenny McLean
Pamela McLellan
Edie Amelia McLoughlin
Helen McNamara
Jeanette Mearns
Pauline Medlyn
Dorothy Meekins
Jacqueline Mecks
Judith Meese
Lynn Mellor
Sarah Mellor
Janet Melvin
Margaret E Mercer
Helen Mervill
Martene Midwood
Carol Millar
Louise Miller
Margaret Caroline Miller
Jo-Ann Millington
Anne Mills
Margaret A Mills
Nancy Millward
Milwich WI
Lauren Misiukanis

Miskin and Mwyndy WI
Sarah Mitchard
E Rae Mitchell (née Cleverly)
Liz Mitchell
Sue Mitchell
Betty Mobbs
Julie Moldon
Eve Mole
Lynn Moralee
June Moran
Roseann Moreno
Joy Morgan
Margaret Morgan
Melody Morgan
Pat Morgan
Sandra Morgan
Sue Morgan
Susan Morgan
Helen Joyce Morris
Margaret Catherine Morris
Claire Morrison
Samantha Mosedale
Anne Moss
Hilary Mullineux
Jeanette Muncey
Munslow WI
Georgina Murmann
Susan Murphy
Liz Muston
Hazel Nation
Jennifer Naylor
Anne Neal
Sylvia J Neal
Susan Neale
Linda Neech
Joan Needham
Mary E Needs
Rosemary Nesbitt
Sheila E Netley
Rachel Neudegg
Sylvia Newall
Connie Newman
Kathleen M Newman
Kathryn Turner Newman
Linda Newton-Griffiths
Helen Nicholson
JA Nicholson
Wendy Nightingale
Jeanette Noble
Ann Noel
Mildred North
North Waltham WI
Norton Lees WI
Carol Elizabeth Nunn
Hilary Nunn
Doreen Mary Nurden
Adzovi Nyanyo
Angela J O'Dell
Elizabeth O'Hea
Fiona O'Leary
Sheila Elizabeth O'Shaughnessy
Ann O'Sullivan
Georgina Oldham
Beatrice Oliver
Evelyn Oliver
Victoria Oliver
Nicola Olway
Estelle M Omand
Alma Oram

S Orgar
Ishbel Orme
Beryl Orton
Barbara Osborn
Elisabeth Osborn
Iris Jessie Osborne
Sheila Oswald
Joanne Ottley
Rosemary Oughton
Sue Ovenden
Phyllis M Owen
Oxfordshire
    Federation of WIs
Veronica Packham
Pamela
    Pakenham-Walsh
Doreen I Palmer
Sylvia Papworth
Sue Pareas
Carol May
    Parker-Kempson
Betty Parker
Hilary Parker
Heather Parks
Sybil Partridge
Marjorie Pascoe
Rita Pateman
Mercia Paterson
Primrose Patey
Maureen Patterson
Pauline Pattison
DM Pavey
Alison Pearce
Jean Letitia Pearce
Lydia Pears
Freda Pearson
Susan Peck
Shirley Pecover
Helen Pendery
Penderyn WI
Muriel Pendlington
Phyllis Penfold
Dawn Penn
Josephine Penn
Alison Penny
Sylvia Perkins
Tina Perkins
Liz Perry
JC Peters
Julia Peters
Patricia Peters
Joan Phelan
Christine Phillips
Connie Phillips
Jane Pickering
M Pickering
Wendy Pickersgill
Yvonne Pickersgill
Dorothy Pike
Margaret
    Pilkington
Barbara Piper
Sandra Pitcher
Hazel Plant
Anne Player
V Plumb
Fay Plummer
Sheila Ponder
Pool in Wharfedale
    WI
Christine Poole
Josie Portas
Muriel Porter
Portesham WI
Portland WI
Patricia Potter
Valerie Potter
Christine Pounder

Margaret Ann
    Power
Betsy Pratty
Alan Preece
Olive M Preston
June Prew
Cheryl Price
Sue Price
Jean Pring
Josephine Prior
Patricia Dorothy
    Prior
Nina Probyn
Gillian Profit
Dorothy Proietti
Maureen Proud
Maralyn
    Pryke-Davies
Ann Purdy
Mary Pycock
Lynne Race
Linda Rachel
Janet Raine
Pauline Rainey
Gillian Anne Ralph
Audrey Read
Gerry Read
Prudence Margaret
    Read
Redberth and
    District WI
Lorraine
    Reed-Wenman
Yvonne H Rees
Doreen Reeve
Emma Regan
Louise Reid
Renhold WI
Margaret Rennison
Helen Revell
Janet Reynolds
Linda Reynolds
Patricia Reynolds
Sue Reynolds
Margaret Rhodes
Maxine Rhodes
June Richards
GM Richardson
Monica Richardson
Dawn Rickatson
Susan Deborah
    Riddle
Betty Ridout
Gillian Rigby
Judith Rigden
Jean Rimmer
Ringmer Evening
    WI
Juliet Rinkel
Ripponden with
    Rishworth WI
Charlotte Roberts
Felicity Roberts
J Roberts
Jennifer Roberts
Joan Robertson
Jacquie Robinson
Pam Robinson
Rhiannon Roderick
Celia Rogers
Irene Margaret
    Rogers
Jean M Rogers
Lesley Rogers
Tracy-Lee Rogers
Ruby Rollo
Romanby WI
J Rome

Rookley WI
Maureen Roose
GC Rose
Jacqueline Honor
    Rose
Dr Suzanna Rose
Muriel Ross-Sharp
Eileen Rosson
Kay Rothery
Mary Rowe
Irene Roxburgh
Catherine Rusby
Angela Rushton
Jane Rushton
Ruskington WI
Helen Russell
Mary Patricia
    Russell
Phillida Russell
Susan Russen
Jean Ryan
Constance Dora
    Rylatt
In memory of Agnes
    Salter
Deborah Sanders
Sandon WI
Pam Sangster
Sawston WI
Judy Saxby
Terri Scanes
Joyce Schaffer
Denise Scott
Caryl M Screaton
Jeanette Seales
Jean Sear
Caroline Elizabeth
    Selby
Mary Selby
Vivienne Selier
Susan Sellars
Linda Sellers
Sandra Senior
Julie Serjeant
Sevenhampton and
    District WI
Shirley Seymour
L Sharman
Cecilia M Sharp
Joyce Sharp
Marjorie Sharp
Shirley Sharp
Rose Sharples
Lesley Shaw
Marguerite Shaw
    (née Sutton)
Mary Sheldon
Suzanne Sheldon
Shepley WI
June Margaret
    Sherlock
Gillian Shilham
Shipston-on-Stour
    WI
Shottlegate and
    District WI
Siddington with
    Preston WI
Maggie Simons
Anne Simpson
Susan E Simpson
Sir Gâr
    Carmarthenshire
    Federation of WIs
Christine Skillicorn
Daphne Skinner
Dorothy Skinner
Dorrie Slade

Slaithwaite WI
Alison Slater
Audrey Smith
Brenda Smith
Brenda Smith
Bridget Smith
Carole Smith
Christine Smith
Colette Smith
Jane Smith
Janet Susan Smith
Jeannette Smith
Linda Smith
Maureen Smith
Patricia G Smith
Shirley Smith
Glenda Smithard
Pauline M Sneddon
Rosemary Snelgrove
Carol Snell
Sue Snook
Valeria Sofar
SE Sorrell
South Wonston WI
Sowerby WI
Barbara Spalding
Fiona Spencer
Patricia Spencer
Kirsty Spreadbury
Gwendoline M
    Sprunt
St Clears WI
Daphne St John
St Mellons WI
St Saviour WI
Jo M Stacey
Elizabeth
    Staddon-Smith
M Staines
Anne Stamper
Dorothea Park
    Standley
Stanwell WI
Rosemary E Stark
Staunton Harold WI
Sue Steele
Steeple Claydon WI
Rosemary Stenning
Katherine Joan
    Stephens
Molly Stephens
Jeanette Stevenson
Nancy Stevenson
Yvonne Stevenson
Jane Stewart
Fiona Stewart-Cox
Steyning Downland
    WI
Suzanne Stickels
Stoborough WI
Rita D Stock
Rosemary Stocker
Valerie Stockley
Mary Stockton
Caroline Stoddart
CR Stone
Jeryl Stone
Heather Stopps
Stretton-on-
    Dunsmore WI
Lynne Stubbings
Diana Such
Aileen Sugars
Anna Sugden
Joyce Sullivan
Ratna Summers
Kathleen
    Sunderland

Denise Surey
Margaret
    Sutherland
Patricia Sutton
Sue Swain
Swainby and Potto
    WI
KM Swainson
Swalecliffe with
    Chestfield WI
Alison Swanson
Gillian Swift
Sheila Swift
Dorothy Sykes
Tracy Sykes
Katy Symon
Diana Szelke
Beatrice M Tapson
Anne Taylor
Barbara Taylor
Barbara Taylor
Beryl Taylor
Hazel Taylor
Joy E Taylor
Joyce Taylor
Mary Taylor
Catherine M
    Tebbitts
Gill Tester
Maureen J Thomas
Maureen J Thomas
Sue Thomas
Eryl Thompsett
Barbara Thompson
Rita Thomson
Kate Thorlby-Coy
Kathleen Thornhill
Josephine Thornton
Tina Thorpe
Lynne Threadgill
Paula Threlfall
Thursby WI
Jane Marianne
    Thwaites
Tibberton and
    Taynton WI
Barbara Tierney
Christine H Tilbury
Liz Tipping
Mildred Tomlinson
Fran Torode
Margaret Towl
    (née Lane)
Diane Towndrow
Elaine Toyer
Dorothy Tozer
Trapp WI
Tremont WI
Gloria Trevarton
Ann Tricker
Daphne Tucker
Jan Tucker
Christine E Tugwell
Jenny Turner
Myrtle Turner
Valeria Turner
Sue Tweddle
Wendoline Twist
Ann Tyler
Denise Tyro
Tytherington WI
Mary Valentine
Kathleen
    Vendervelde
Helen Marie
    Vaughan
Jill Vaughan
Jude Vaughan

Jennifer Ann
    Vincent
Sandra J Vizer
Marion Wade
Margaret Waghorn
Sue Wake
Beverley
    Wakeford-Brown
Audrey Walker
Betty May Walker
Eileen E Walker
Elizabeth Walker
Liz Walker
Gillian M Wall
Jenny Wall
Pamela Wallace
Anne Walshaw
Deborah Walton
Angie Ward
Dorothy Ward
Joanne Ward
Joyce Ann Ward
Lisa Rougier Ward
Pat Ward
Muriel Wardle
Wardy Hill WI
Janet Warne
Valerie C Warr
Jane Warren
Muriel Wasley
Amanda Wason
Stella Waterer
Jean Waters
Sue Watkins
Catherine Watson
Katherine Watson
Katherine F Watson
Margaret Watson
Liz Watt
Vivien Watt
Sharon Anne Wayte
Maggie Weatherby
Eluned Webb
Ruth Webb
Ann Webber
Ann Webster
Diane Webster
Eileen Webster
PA Weetman
Jean J Weightman
Wellesbourne WI
Wellingore WI
Barbara Wells
Deirdre Wells
Julia Wells
M Wells
Valerie Floreen
    Wells
Welney WI
Ruth Welsh
Evelyn Welsman
Wendover Evening
    WI
West Sussex
    Federation of WIs
West Yorkshire
    Federation of WIs
Sarah Westaby
Diana Weston
Lorrie Westwood
Christine E Whaley
    JP
Linda A Whatman
Linda Wheat
Floss Wheatley
Mary Wheaton
Dorothy M Wheeler
Marian F Wheeler

Peggy Wheeler
Hilary White
Grace Whitehouse
Gail Whitehurst
Sylvia Whiter
Sue Whitfield
Vanessa Whitley
Yolande Whitley
Beryl Whitty
Jill Whybrow
Siân Whyte
Rosemary
    Wibberley
Wigginton and
    Haxby WI
Mary Wildman
Roz Wiley
ML Wilkins
Sheila Wilkins
Pauline Willcox
Betty Williams
Carys Williams
Diana Williams
Dot Williams
Janet Williams
Judith Williams
Marion Williams
Mary Williams
Norma Williams
Pamela Williams
Rachel Morgan
    Williams
Sylvia Margaret
    Williams
Yvonne Williams
Libbi Williamson
Nancy Willingon
Catherine Elizabeth
    Willmott
Barbara Wills
Doreen Wilson
Julia Dawn Wilson
K Jean Wilson
Susan Peta Wilson
Wenda Wilson
Kathleen Winslow
Margaret AS
    Winterbourne
Witney WI
Margaret Wood
Tracey Wood
Pat Woodall
Sue Woodford
Susan Woodham
Gail Wooliscroft
Frances Woollam
Susan Woollard
Joan Woolmington
Anne Wooster
Wootton Wawen
    WI
Gill Workman
Worlaby WI
Worlingworth and
    Tannington WI
June Wreford
Becky Wright
Brenda Wright
Carole Wright
Momena Wright
Sarah L Wright
Sylvia Wynands
Yardley Gobion WI
Hazel Yate
Eileen Lawson Yeo
Maureen Yeowell
Margaret RA Young
Pauline Zaccardelli

Index